Elk Hunting 101

A Pocketbook Guide to Elk Hunting

Jay Houston

Colorado Elk Camp
America's #1 Online Resource for Elk Hunters

www.elkcamp.com

Jackson Creek Publishers
Colorado Springs, Colorado 80920

ELK HUNTING 101,
A POCKETBOOK GUIDE TO ELK HUNTING

That grand bull elk on our cover is courtesy of Jerry Taylor.
If you like his work and want to contact Jerry, you can email him at:
jerry@wildintherockies.com.

Back cover photo of Jay Houston by Roger Medley

Inside photos by: Jerry Taylor, Jay Houston, Roger Medley
and Mike Byrd

Printed in the United States of America

ISBN 0-9759319-0-3

CONTENTS

How to use this book

Elk Hunting 101 is designed to serve as a pocket field manual. I have formatted it with extra wide outside margins on each page so that you can take it with you into the field and jot down notes of your own. Learning is a life long experience. I find that the older I get the more I want to keep notes. So I encourage you to mark this up. It will become a more useful resource for the effort.

You will notice that I have included quite a few practical **Tips** on elk hunting. These are identified by **bold** print. The idea that anyone could or should memorize the entire content of a book is ridiculous, so I have chosen easy to remember tidbits that I believe can help you to become a more knowledgeable and more successful elk hunter.

Finally, it is important to keep in mind that *Elk Hunting 101* is fundamental level field guide. While it is written to equip elk hunters of all skill levels, its focus is on supplying elk hunters and future elk hunters with the "basics."

In *Elk Hunting 201*, due out in 2005, I will delve even deeper into the depths of elk hunting discussing such subjects as: elk hunting tactics and strategies, the ultimate setup, where to find big bulls, successfully hunting elk on public land; how to reduce the weight and bulk of your elk hunting gear by half and still be successful, and much more.

Acknowledgements

Were it not for the contributions and support of many others, whether friend or family works such as this would never see the light of day. As a writer it is essential that I give credit to those who made this possible. In that regard I want to give huge credit to:

My Lord and Savior Jesus Christ, who through His grace released my heart from bondage and equipped me with the talent, experience, patience, and courage to write this book.

My love Rae Ann whose continuous encouragement kept me at this project until it was finished, and whose unselfish love makes it possible for me to spend time in the high country observing, hunting, and learning more about elk.

My parents. To Dad who took me on my first hunt and patiently showed me the way, and to Mom who has always encouraged me to pursue my dreams. I love you both forever.

Some great American elk hunters and lovers of the adventure of being a part of God's great outdoors without whose input this volume would be so much less: Mike Byrd, Roger & Shasta Medley, Josh Byrd, Aaron Monroe, Tim Jones, Chris Jeub, Steve Chapman, Randy & Jeanne Horne, Larry & Melody Money, Wayne Carlton, Sandy Whitaker, Tracy, Breen, and Phil Weaver

Finally but most assuredly not the least, the memory of my grand friend, mentor, brother in Christ, and faithful elk huntin' buddy, Angus (Rex) Gardner. Lynn thanks for sharing Rex with me for a time. I look forward to seeing you again my brother.

INTRODUCTION

As a die-hard elk hunter who takes the opportunity to participate in the grand adventure of elk hunting very seriously, I believe that there are five key factors that if applied with determination, will result in a successful elk hunt.

1) Gain a comprehensive and practical knowledge of the elk.
2) Craft a well thought out and comprehensive plan for your hunt, remembering to build in a bit of flexibility.
3) Commit your willpower and ability to endure the rigors of elk hunting in the face of adverse conditions and circumstances.
4) Have the patience of Job.
5) Execute effective hunting tactic, i.e. follow your plan…and pray.

Folks, becoming a successful elk hunter is not a rocket science. It does, however, require the average hunter to be willing to plan diligently, work hard, and make some sacrifices. If you are not prepared to do all of the above with vigor, save yourself some time and give this book to a friend now, because without this level of commitment, nothing you may glean from this book is going to make any difference. To the best of my 35 plus years of big game hunting knowledge, there are no "cookbook" solutions to successful elk hunting.

Elk Hunting 101 will provide valuable insight to elk hunters of all experience levels into the fundamentals of what is required to become an effective and successful hunter of this great animal.

Elk hunting is dynamic. By this I mean that those factors that may affect the outcome of your hunt are always in a state of change. The weather, terrain, wind, hunting pressure, and the habits of the elk themselves are nearly always in a constant state of transition. The successful elk hunter willingly acknowledges this, and builds a plan that takes into account all of these dynamics and about a dozen more.

Finally, don't look for a checklist that if completed successfully, will result in a Boone and Crocket Club® bull hanging on the wall. This book is about preparation and performance. If adhered to, these guidelines and suggestions can "help" you become a better and hopefully more successful elk hunter. If I had to summarize the focus of this book, I would use an old saying from my days in the military:

" Prior Preparation Prevents
Poor Performance."

Photo: 1 Summer Bachelor Bull

Chapter 1

Do your Elk Hunting Homework

The following discussion on homework is my executive summary of the entire book. It is designed for those who want answers fast. For the life of me, I cannot understand why someone would buy a book if they didn't want to read it through, but reality being what it is; I thought that I would include this overview. Perhaps reading it will stir something within and keep your interest long enough for you to read the entire book and glean the information that cannot be discussed in such a summary.

At my website, www.elkcamp.com, I get visitors from all parts of the country and beyond for lots of reasons. During 1996, our first year online, I discovered that the single area that got the most hits was our "Elk Camp Hunter's Forum." During the months of July - October on average we received nearly 1,000 hits per day (back then I thought this was a lot), and most of these were from hunters like you asking one question, where are the elk? In response many of you offered tips to help your fellow hunters by getting them pointed in the right direction without giving away the exact location of that back country bowl or hidden bench.

Unfortunately, I have no crystal ball, but by spending a little time gaining a working understanding of elk behavior, elk needs, and following a few general guidelines almost anyone can locate elk in that big expanse of wilderness called... elk country.

Years ago a good friend shared the following acrostic with me. For those of you wanting to know how to scout for and locate elk, this is my absolute best tip.

Tip #1. Prior Preparation Prevents Poor Performance.

In other words do your homework. Much of your potential for success in elk hunting will depend upon: 1) spending plenty of pre-season time scouting the ground you intent to hunt, and 2) getting yourself into shape. If you want to shortcut these recommendations, you need to be willing to pay outfitter big bucks to do your homework for you. Either way someone has to do the homework. As for 3), take it from one who has been there, most elk country is big and tough and will promptly kick your backside if you are not mentally and physically prepared to deal with it.

How much effort do you need to put into getting into shape? Think of it as trying out for the high school football team... only those in the best of shape will be able to survive, much less achieve their objective of becoming a starting player. The good news is that day one is the toughest. Every day of preparation thereafter, while not exactly easy, will be less trying than the day before as your mind and body get in shape.

You may ask, "I'm young (maybe 40) and in pretty good shape, why should I have to get in shape? Try this. Locate the biggest hill in your area, unless you live in Tibet; load up a day pack with say, a light load of 20 pounds of rocks, and try hiking up and down that hill 4 or 5 times. This is roughly the equivalent of the workout you will get before noon on opening day of elk season here in Colorado. Now how "in shape" do you feel? See my point?

One final thing to consider is altitude. I live in Colorado Springs, which for Colorado is pretty much the lowland at approximately 7,000 feet above sea level. Here in "The Springs," the amount of oxygen available to breathe is about 25% less than that available at sea level, like in most parts of Texas. How can you get a feel for what that reduction in your air supply is like? While your hauling that 20# bag of rocks up that hill, place your hand gently over your mouth and pinch your nose shut altogether. This will restrict your airflow thereby giving you some idea of what it is like hunting at higher elevations. Keep in mind that there are very few elk to be found here in Colorado Springs. Actually, I have seen a few, but most elk are found at higher elevations between 8,000 and 11,000 feet depending on the time of the year and the snow line.

Tip #2: If you want to be successful at elk hunting in Colorado or most any other western state hosting an elk herd, you will need to start getting in shape now.

When I was in school, I hated homework. It taxed me mentally, took time away from other activities (cars and girls) that I would have preferred spending my time on, and as a kid, I could see no practical advantage to doing it. Elk hunting homework is not so different with one very important exception, the practical aspect. If you don't do your homework, your chances of locating elk in the millions of square miles of wilderness are about as good as your chances of your boss saying "why don't you take a few weeks off "on me" to go elk hunting. Possible yes, probable I don't think so. The practical advantage to doing your homework is the assurance that you are as prepared as possible for a successful elk hunt.

In my opinion a successful elk hunt is roughly 15 % hunting skill, 15% luck and 70% first-class preparation. If you don't take time to prepare or if you cheat on this aspect of your hunt, don't be surprised when you go home empty handed.

Guys always want a checklist or something to measure by it's our nature. So you may ask, how much prep is enough? On average I personally spend about ten hours of preparation throughout the year for every one hour actually hunting during elk season. If you figure that I hunt roughly 15 hours per day for 5 days that equates to 75 hours of hunting thus my preparation for the hunt is around 750 hours throughout the year. Yeah…that is a lot of work!

When do I need to start planning my hunt? Each year my elk hunting homework begins not long after the previous season's end. For those of you who like to take notes, here is how I do my homework.

Tip #3: Explore the lessons that you learned on the previous year's hunt.

What worked and what didn't. I try to review every moment of that hunt, from the time we got out in the boonies (woods), to the elevations we hunted, wind direction and speed at various times of the day, time spent sitting and glassing versus time on the move, etc. You know the list. The difference is that I want to remember to repeat those activities that worked and dump or change those that failed to help bring an elk to ground. Why repeat something year after year that doesn't work. As my daughters used to say before they ran off and got married ... duh?

Tip #4: Determine if you will hunt the same area the following year or if you need to move on to another area.

Let me clarify a point here. I hunt public land 100 % of the time for a number of reasons, primarily because I cannot afford to drop $1,500 - $4,000 per season to gain access to private land. Many of those trophy size bulls (350 +) you see in the "hook and bullet" magazines are found on private ranches, while the majority of Colorado's nearly 300,000 head of elk live most of their lives on public land, such as national forests, BLM land, or state land. If you are considering changing hunting areas, some reasons might include: no elk or small numbers of elk in your area, very difficult or inaccessible terrain, or too many orange vests. This last one warrants a brief story.

For years I hunted the same area in Routt County. The area we hunted in had two heavily used access points. Each morning we were all up and heading to our favorite benches, ridges, and holes well before sunrise and every morning for years this, let's say, "older" lady would beat me to what I thought was a great stand. We had talked briefly the first year, but after that every time I saw her orange vest sitting behind that blown down aspen, I would head off in another direction. At first I thought nothing of it, but eventually my curiosity got the better of me as to how she could manage to beat me to this location regardless of how early I got there year after year. So I determined to pay her a call to say hi the following season. Opening day of the second combined rifle season, I headed out to make this call upon my mysterious friend. As I rounded the bend in the old logging road, there she was waiting on me as if we had scheduled this rendezvous. I casually strolled over to her, making certain to let her know I was coming to avoid getting shot. Keep in mind that it is still darker than midnight when I discovered to my surprise, that my friend was now only an orange vest draped carefully over a stump, presumably strategically placed there by someone to give hunters like myself the impression of another hunter. Pretty smart huh? My point here is not that I advocate this type of deception, more so some hunter knew that other hunters would respect and avoid this "occupied" area. It worked! Each year I find more and more hunters a field as evidenced by vehicles, chance encounters, ATV's, but ever more by the herds of orange vests speckling the ridge tops and hill sides. Don't get me wrong. I am a strong hunting advocate, but I just prefer to be off by myself, or at least not in the middle of a crowd.

If I am moving on to a new area, the real work begins. How do you determine if one area is than better than another? To answer this question, you have to become somewhat of a detective. What you are looking for is information, the most valuable commodity on the planet! So don't expect to get it without making a personal investment and keep in mind that anything of value doesn't come cheap.

Some good resources to start with are fellow hunters, Colorado Division of Wildlife officers, Forest Service rangers, landowners, the Internet, and CDOW's annual hunting stats booklet. One thing to keep in mind when you want to strike up a conversation with any of the above, "when in Rome...." If you want to initiate a two-way dialogue with someone, particularly a dialogue where you expect them to provide you with their information, you need to make them feel comfortable about talking with you, be one of the boys. Leave the $400 cowboy boots and $200 sweaters at home, and avoid talking about "what you think" since most people, except those closest to you, don't really care what you think anyhow. Everyone, and I mean everyone, sooner or later likes to talk about themselves, so let them... while casually steering the conversation in the direction you would like it to go, specifically towards elk hunting.

Again, this does not imply that one should be deceptive. I believe that honesty is by far the best policy, but a reasonable amount of tact and common sense is required if you want to learn something from this individual. One good source for these types of contacts is the local diner or coffee shop. Here, though skeptical of strangers, most folks are a bit more relaxed and willing to share. They also feel secure on their own turf. Focus on that word... share. Any such discussion should be a two way street. Perhaps you have some information of value for your contact. At least offer to buy the meal or coffee. Never take and run. Show genuine interest in what the other fellow has to say. One of the best icebreakers is to start off with common ground. Maybe you know someone in town. Feel free to share a "war story" of yours about this common acquaintance. Chances are that if you are in elk country, your contact already has something in common with you, elk hunting! Finally, never dive directly into the part of the conversation about where to hunt. This means that you should treat him or her with the same respect that you would want to be treated with.

Let me briefly touch on statistics. As we all know, anyone can make a set of statistics "talk", and make a convincing argument. The key to reliable statistics is the validity of the research that went into producing the data. DOW is not going to like this next remark, and someone there is sure to read this and I'll likely catch you know what for it, but sources within the Division have been overheard (first hand) to say that some herd stats published for public consumption are at times the figment of a game management officers imagination, calculated to present a predetermined political objective for the individual or area. With that said, these stats are a fair source of information, but should be verified with a bit of personal detective work interviewing locals.

Tip #5: Once you have determined to move on, you've interviewed some good resources, and found a prospective new area, it's time to get out the topo maps.

Topographical maps come in a variety of forms and scales. Ultimately, you will want to use a map that will provide you with a good picture including significant detail on the area you plan to hunt. There are a number of good topo map books on the market, like *Delorme's Colorado Atlas & Gazetteer* (scale 1:160,000 to 1:320,000) available for around $17.00 that will allow you to get started with this process. The new editions also include GPS data for those of you more technologically inclined. If you are considering using a GPS, check out *GPS Made Easy* by Lawrence Letham published by The Mountaineers Press available in your local bookstore. Once you have narrowed your hunt area to within say 16 square miles (4 miles by 4 miles) you will want to head on over to your local supplier of USGS quad maps. Better yet you can design, construct and purchase your own custom Quad at our website www.elkcamp.com. These maps reflect a scale of 1:24,000 or 1:25,000 and show the greatest amount of detail. You can also obtain larger scale maps from the US Forest Service or the Bureau of Land Management for a small fee. These maps generally fit in the former category of those maps good to start with and get a general feel for the lay of the land.

For those unfamiliar with map reading and the use of a good compass, there are numerous books at your local library or sporting goods supply store to help you acquire these skills, which are an "absolute" if you want to survive in elk country. One great reference source is *Be Expert With Map & Compass, The Complete Orienteering Handbook* by Bjorn Hjellstom. If you prefer classroom like instruction, many of the larger sporting goods chains and backpack supply outlets offer "orienteering" courses. These usually last a few hours and will equip you with enough basic orienteering skills to keep you out of all but extreme trouble.

Tip #6: Most hunters on public land hunt within 1 mile of a road. Why, because they are either lazy, physically limited, or afraid of getting lost. Hint folks-elk are not stupid and know to avoid these congested areas during hunting season. If you want to locate more elk, you need to be willing and prepared to get away from the roads.

That is not to say one cannot hunt near roads, just that your chances of killing anything while hunting near them are considerably less, which brings to mind another story I heard which blows this theory all to pieces, but it's a great tale.

Some guys were hunting national forest land in Routt county a few years back during the second combined rifle season. There were two or three other elk camps in close proximity to theirs, all within a half mile of a state highway. In one of the other camps, a fellow hunter had brought his wife along for company. She however preferred to remain in camp and read rather than traipse about all day like the rest of the hunters. Each day this lady would place her lawn chair on the edge of their camp and read and watch smaller wildlife while cars and trucks passed by her on the state road. Imagine their surprise one afternoon when they came back to camp and found this little old lady sitting in her chair with this big, you know what kind, grin on her face. She says, "Would you boys mind helping me for just a minute. I need some help getting that ole' elk up here to camp." "What elk says they?" "That 6x6 bull down yonder in the field by the road." says she." He just walked out of the timber over there by the creek and I just up and shot him with Jim's other rifle." They never did ask her if she had her own license, and I surely do not advocate hunting without one. The lady and her husband were gone the next morning, so that may be the answer to that question. The point here is that from time to time elk can be found just about anywhere. Heck, I was darn near kamakazied by an elk herd one subzero winter morning before sunup standing slap dab in the middle of I-25 just north of the United States Air Force Academy. Just goes to show you, but keep in mind...most elk are a bit more difficult to locate, so be prepared to work for it.

Tip #7: Walk the land.

Many hunters new to an area show up on opening day never having laid eyes on the ground they intend to hunt. In many cases, like hunters from out of state, which make up a significant number of those you will meet these hunters are at a significant disadvantage due to their unfamiliarity with the land. The more familiar one is with the terrain, the location of those hidden benches and holes (valley for folks back East) that hold elk, the migration or travel routes, prevailing wind, sources of food and water, wallows, etc. the higher one's likelihood of putting meat in the freezer. I'll really step out on a limb here and offer that without some amount of pre-season homework, your chances of bringing home a nice bull are about as likely as standing in camp, firing up in the air and hoping the bullet will bring down something. I realize that this is a fairly extreme comparison, but it should serve to get the point across...if you want to be successful at elk hunting, you have got to do your homework...'nough said.

Chapter 2

Elk Huntin' Ain't Deer Huntin'

Growing up in the South, I had the opportunity to hunt everything from bobwhite quail to raccoons and whitetail deer. I've hunted in nearly every Southern state, and you can take my word for it; until the recent elk transplantation efforts of the Rocky Mountain Elk Foundation, there were no elk in the South, at least none that were not already hanging over someone else's fireplace. How is this relevant you may ask? The relevancy is this. Hunting whitetail deer whether in the South, the Midwest, the Northeast, or anywhere else for that matter is a far stretch from elk hunting. Elk Huntin' ain't deer huntin'. For some perspective let's take a look at some of the differences.

Whitetail deer habitat typically ranges from lowland farm country and woodlots to open prairie. Hardwoods like oak, hickory, and maple are common browse for whitetail deer. With few exceptions, whitetails are found at elevations from sea level to about 4,000 feet. Elk on the other hand can be found in open pasture at 5,000 feet, but primarily inhabit much higher and more rugged mountain terrain, covered in a variety of pines and firs as well as aspen, ranging from 8,000 feet to well above timberline and altitudes of 12,000 and greater.

Whitetail deer are primarily browsers, meaning they prefer to eat from the tree or brush as opposed to the ground. Elk, like cattle, prefer to graze on grass, succulents, and other feed found on or very near the ground. Granted, either will shift their feeding preferences depending upon what is available, but their preferences remain the same.

Where deer are far more solitary critters traveling mostly as singles or in smaller groups, elk are herd animals, opting for living and traveling in groups ranging from a few animals to hundreds, Granted, I've seen many elk traveling as singles, but these have been few and far between.

One summer a few years ago, I was invited along on a summer pack trip in the Flat Tops Wilderness area of Colorado, so I decided to combine this opportunity with a little scouting. My hosts were Randy and Jeanne Horne owners of Bar-H Outfitters (www.barhoutfitters.com) in Meeker, CO. It was early July, so the bulls and cows were mostly split up at this time. The ride in took maybe three hours, but in the course of perhaps one of those hours on horseback, we saw and filmed what we reasonably estimated at between 600 and 700 head of elk, all traveling in large groups of 50-300. This is not to say that one can expect to see groups of this size regularly. It is to reinforce my point that elk travel primarily in groups.

I wish I could tell you how many times I've heard some hunter say, "There ain't no elk around here." Well, maybe there are and maybe there are not. Any given area may hold a quantity of elk, but if a hunter doesn't know how to maximize his chances of locating these elk, he is likely to respond similarly. So how can a hunter "maximize his opportunity of seeing elk?"

Tip #8: The key is to cover as much ground as possible.

Try to picture this. You are hunting an area that is approximately 2 miles square, i.e. 2 miles by 2 miles and is known to hold 100 animals. Granted this is a rather small area but for purposes of this example, just bear with me. Conventional deer hunting strategy says look for game trails, signs, or areas that would provide a source of food or water, and set up a stand. Your stand might be a tree stand, a ground blind, or just hiding behind a tree. Either way, you have done your homework and now you have staked out a point of ambush, right? Well maybe, but probably not. Why? As I mentioned earlier, deer travel in singles and small groups so the probability of one of those hundred deer inhabiting the two square mile area walking somewhere close to your stand are fairly good, but lets consider the travel patterns of elk. Remember, elk travel in herds. Here I will be conservative and assume that the same 100 animals (elk) are moving about in the same two mile square area. If the same hunter sets himself up in the same stationary blind, what do you think his chances are of seeing these elk that may all be traveling together or in a few family groups. Let's say that the stand is over a wallow on the edge of a small meadow that is 500 yards long and 500 yards wide, which is fairly large as some go. All it takes is for the elk herd to pass you in the dark timber by a few yards. Believe me, you would be surprised how quiet a herd of elk can be tip toeing through the woods and causing you to miss the entire event. If you are honest, you'll admit that a hunter's chances of locating the elk from a stationary stand are significantly less than his chances would have been for locating deer. So how do I hunt elk? I'll talk about that more in the chapter on methods of elk hunting.

Chapter 3

Where Did All the Oxygen Go?

As I mentioned in the previous chapter, elk range in the Rockies is typically found at relatively high altitudes compared to sea level. I live in Colorado Springs, 60 miles south of Denver, which has an elevation above sea level of approximately 7,000 feet. Some of you reading this may say, I've never even seen anything 7,000 high before. Heck, many years ago when I lived in North Carolina, the highest point in the state was just over 4,000 feet and that was in the Appalachians. Now I sit at my desk writing at almost twice that elevation.

Basic high school science taught us that as we ascend in altitude, the amount of available oxygen decreases, i.e. the higher you go, the less oxygen you have to breathe. Back when I was flying, we learned that there is something called a "Standard Lapse Rate." Standard lapse rate says that in addition to some other things, as you ascend in altitude the amount of available oxygen decreases at a fixed rate. I wish I could tell you exactly what that rate is, but if it interests you that much, I'm sure you can find that information on the Internet or in a library. Suffice it to say that as I sit here at my desk in Colorado Springs, that the amount of available oxygen to breath is between 25 and 30 percent less that anyone else sitting at their desk at sea level, say in New Orleans. The point that I hope to make in this chapter is that in order to plan for a successful elk hunt in the Rockies, every hunter will need to understand the adverse effects and consequences of the significantly reduced amount of available oxygen at the elevations in which elk live.

Before I begin to tell you about all the negative effects of hunting at higher altitudes, I will offer one word of encouragement for those who, despite their best efforts, will find the lack of oxygen slowing them down. A friend of mine, Wayne Carlton (inventor of the diaphragm elk call), in one of his elk hunting videos, states that as he gets older he finds that he cannot climb mountains with the same vigor that he did when he was younger.

Tip #9: As a result of slowing down a bit, Wayne sees more elk every year. I agree wholeheartedly with Wayne. As I have aged, I have slowed down as well and similarly, I see more elk too.

Well Wayne, we may be older (not old), but we are getting better.

If you want to maximize your potential for a successful elk hunt, you will need to come to grips with how you are going to prepare for and deal with having less available oxygen to keep you going from long before sunrise to sunset, and maybe thereafter. Your ability to effectively manage this will be key to your success. Should you choose to disregard this key issue, it may play a deciding role in your failure to locate elk. The following are what I believe are three key factors that every hunter who is not used to living and working hard at higher altitudes should consider in his planning for a successful elk hunt. For those of you who do live at or above 5,000 feet, now would be a good time to take a break, stretch your legs, and get a cup of coffee. For the rest of you:

First, get in shape. I'll cover this topic more in the chapter on endurance, but for now you will want to:

Tip #10: Build a plan that will prepare your body, specifically your lungs and cardio vascular system, for working longer and harder with less oxygen

Don't make the mistake like so many who have come before you of thinking that you can wait until August and then begin taking leisurely strolls around the block or the park, and expect to get in shape. Such a workout regimen would probably prepare you for being the camp cook, but I can assure you, it will fall far short of preparing your lungs for what can realistically be a 14 - 20 hour day of humping up and down mountains with a rifle or bow and whatever other gear you carry. I suggest that you begin with a light cardio workout and then gradually increase the length and difficulty of your workout. This can be running, power walking, or jogging on the treadmill. In my opinion, for those who can afford one, a treadmill is the ultimate cardio trainer, especially those that can be programmed to simulate an uphill grade. These will vary your workout in speed and angle, which will help strengthen not only your cardio vascular system, but also those oh-so-important thigh, calf, and ankle muscles, which are critical for endurance in hunting the Rockies. Treadmills also have the added value of being resistant to weather in that they are usually indoors. This will allow you to maintain your workout schedule regardless of the weather.

Ok, so now we have a written schedule for getting ourselves in shape. When do I need to begin? My answer is an emphatic now! Hopefully you are not reading this the week before elk season kicks off, but if you are, get off your backside and take this book for a long walk today! Really, each individual will require a different level of preparation, but on average, I suggest that you do the following.

Tip #11: Begin your training a minimum of three months prior to your planned hunt date.

For some this may be less. If you are what a personal trainer would say is in good or better cardio vascular shape, if you are well within the median of your weight range for your height and age, you may be able to reduce this lead time. As I am not a professional trainer, I strongly suggest that you consult your personal physician before beginning any type of exercise or workout.

Another suggestion for getting in shape is that in addition to everything else, you should

Tip #12: Carry a backpack with you on your workout.

When I was flying in fighters in the Air National Guard, we were constantly training. One of our mottos was "train like you expect to fight." This means that we should

Tip #13: Work diligently to ensure that our training program closely simulates what we expect to encounter in the real world.

To this end, the purpose of the backpack suggestion should become obvious. While hunting, you will be carrying your day gear, i.e. food, survival gear, water, extra socks, etc. in some type of pack. It is not important whether you choose to carry a backpack or a fanny pack. What is important is that either will add extra weight that you will have to deal with during your hunt and you should train for this appropriately. I suggest that when you begin your training program you put a few rocks in the pack and that as you progress through your training you continue to add more rocks so that by the end of your training program, the weight of your pack will actually exceed that weight that you expect to carry on your hunt. That way, when you head out into the boonies, not only will your cardio vascular system be ready, but so will your back and neck muscles.

Tip #14: If you are a smoker...quit!

Don't tell yourself the lie that you can quit anytime that you want and wait until a few weeks before season. That is a crock! Quit today, right now, this second. Put the book down, go find every cigarette in the house, crush them, and trash them. Now go tell everyone you know (this is important) that you have decided to quit smoking today, and that you want them to help you "stay the course," and to hold you accountable for your decision. Folks, I'm not just blowing smoke here, no pun intended, I am an ex-smoker. I started smoking with the other boys on my block when I was fourteen and smoked until I was thirty. By then, I had seen enough of how smoking can destroy one's body and severely limit one's ability to enjoy life. I had a family who would miss out on a lot if I continued to destroy my life with tobacco. So I quit cold turkey. Without going into all the details, there are many ways today to kick the habit, and cold turkey is surely not the easiest. It is a true test of one's will, determination, and desire to have a better life.

If you find yourself in this category, i.e. a smoker who wants to quit, here is my personal suggestion for quitting. It may or may not work for you. It did work for me. I looked into the eyes of my family and found there something that was far more valuable, far more meaningful to me than the high that comes from nicotine. I found in their eyes and their smiles something I wanted and needed more, their love and affirmation. Folks, there was no competition. I knew that if I were to continue to smoke, the adverse affects would in all likelihood be devastating to their lives as well, so I quit.

Tip #15: I found something more important, more valuable. I determined that a lasting relationship with my family was worth the fight.

I have a huntin' buddy. Actually, I have a lot of guys that I hunt with who are great friends, hunters, and buddies, but there is one in particular that I refer to, actually we do it mutually, as one of my huntin' buddies (it's a long story), Phil Weaver, aka. Ol'Arky. Phil was a smoker until his heart attack in 2002. Today Phil is a "believer and ex-smoker."

Phil and I actually met via my online hunter's discussion forum at Colorado Elk Camp, a great place to ask questions about elk hunting and swap stories with others who have become addicts to this sport. Our discussion led to the discovery of similar interest and backgrounds, which led to my flying from Colorado Springs to Memphis and then driving four hours to Phil's part of Arkansas to meet this die hard elk and duck hunter that I had only known via an online discussion group and some phone calls. Phil wanted to show me "his Arkansas elk herd." He didn't actually say that, but I could tell that as a resident of Arkansas, he was proud of what his home state of Arkansas and the Rocky Mountain Elk Foundation had done to reintroduce elk to the Buffalo River valley.

Phil is a good-natured grizzly looking fellow and upon meeting him for the first time, I could tell we would become good friends. I recall that first day, searching for the elk herd of the Buffalo River valley, telling tales of past hunts, and building dreams of future hunts together. I also remember one other aspect of Phil's character that stuck out and admittedly caused me some rather serious concern. Phil smoked, not just a little, but a lot, like a steam engine. I remember thinking to myself, how does this guy handle the altitude of hunting the Colorado Rockies, much less ever see an elk, and be a smoker. Don't get me wrong, and Phil when you read this, please forgive me huntin' buddy, this was not a character judgment, it was merely a question. How does he do it?

The following fall, Phil and his lovely wife Linda drove 22 hours from Arkansas to our base camp at 10,500 feet high in the Rockies. For nearly a week, Phil hunted just as long and as hard as everyone else, a testament to his determination, but it was clear that the damage to his lungs from years of smoking was taking its toll. Is Phil any less of a great elk hunter, absolutely not! Do I think that Phil had to work harder than the rest of our group, you bet! While a heart attack is a fearsome and terrible event in anyone's life, it can be, and was in Phil's case, a wake up call. Today, Phil is an ex-smoker. If you want to know what he thinks about this subject, you'll have to ask him. To smoke or not to smoke, the choice is up to you. Give 'em up or be prepared to suffer and work three times as hard at elk hunting as every non-smoker in camp. And also be prepared to sleep in a tent of your own.

Chapter 4

Endurance... An Absolute for the Successful Elk Hunter

My absolute favorite definition of endurance is one's determination and ability to stay the course. This breaks down into three separate aspects: Determination or what I like to call the mind game; Ability – the physical; and finally Stay the Course – or Direction. All three are key ingredients in one's plan for a successful elk hunt. The omission of any of these elements leaves a hole in your strategy big enough for an entire herd of elk to escape through. Let's look at each of these in a bit more detail.

Determination – The mind game of successful elk hunting

If you want to be successful in the field at elk hunting, one of the first challenges you will need to deal with is getting your head on straight. You must decide upon your level of commitment to the task. You've probably heard the story about the chicken and the pig as it applies to one's level of commitment, but for purposes of this discussion I think it bears repeating here.

A pig and a chicken are standing out in the barnyard talking one morning when they see the farmer's wife through the kitchen window preparing to fix the morning breakfast. While the chicken is pretty much care free, talking a mile a minute, the pig is somewhat quiet with a worried look on his face. After some time the chicken realizes that he is involved in a one-way conversation and asks the pig what is wrong? The pig looks at the chicken and says, "Can't you see what she is doing? She is fixing breakfast in there. Doesn't that bother you?" The chicken looks over his shoulder at the farmer's wife, and then looks back to the pig. "Why should her fixing breakfast bother me?" "For heaven's sake man, she's fixing ham and eggs! Can't you see that, says the pig. Eggs come from chickens and ham comes from pigs." "Yea, so what's the big deal? What's the difference, asks the chicken." "Well I'll tell you says the pig. She's fixing ham and eggs. As a chicken you are just involved, but as a pig, I am totally committed!"

Over the years, I've run across almost every type of elk hunter that you can imagine. First there is "Weekend William." This is the guy who grabs his brand new elk rifle, hops in his $40,000 4x4 pickup and heads out into the high country for one weekend (maybe less) a year. This guy gives little to no thought to planning, scouting, gear, or knowledge of the elk. Rest assured that he has however, seen

every elk video ever produced in the comfort
of his living room. Out of 365 days, his total
annual elk hunting experience will be
completed in 48 hours or less. No mess, no
fuss, and back home in time for Sunday
dinner. Since luck often plays a large part in
any successful elk hunt, this guy has just as
much "chance" as anyone else. My guess is
that the only thing this hunter is going to bring
home is a dirty pickup. This is what I call
extremely marginal commitment.

Next there is "Hopeful Harry." Harry
has a heart for hunting. He grew up hunting
with his dad, uncles, and brothers somewhere
in the South or Midwest. Harry has been a
successful whitetail hunter for most of his life
and has taken the plunge, shelled out a wad of
cash for gear and traveled a thousand miles or
more to elk country to try his hand for the
trophy of a lifetime. Harry has seen all the
videos too. Harry's level of determination
cannot be measured. He is consumed. Harry
has been worked up about this hunt since the
day he saw his first elk hunt on cable TV.
Harry can spell commitment and is starting to
get the idea.

Finally, there is Ed the Elk Hunter. Ed
knows the rules of the game. He has spent
countless hours researching elk characteristics
and habits, studying topographical maps,
talking to anyone and everyone about elk,
scouting the land, and preparing himself
mentally and physically for the challenges of
elk hunting. Ed's determination for a
successful elk hunt began the final day of last
years elk season. For 360 days he has focused
on learning from last years mistakes and
enhancing or acquiring those skills that he

believes will make him a better hunter for the next elk season. Ed's level of commitment and determination for success is off the chart.

Mental Preparation

There will come a point in nearly every elk hunt where your reserves will begin to deplete. It may be on day one, or it may not come until later on in your hunt, but it will happen. Elk hunting is hard work in big country. The days are long. The weather is often cold and sometimes inhospitable. As the days progress, you stink like week old road kill because you haven't had a bath in a week. The food is probably not nearly up to par with what you are used to from home. You may have been living in some cramped space with a bunch of guys who have started to complain about everything from the lack of elk to who bought the industrial grade toilet paper. (Sidebar here folks. Never go cheap on the TP at camp. There is nothing that will ruin a great camp faster than a rash.) This is the point where a successful elk hunter must get his act together and take serious measure of himself. I have never been on an elk hunt where I failed to see this happen to some hunters in camp. As I mentioned earlier, for some it comes sooner, for others later, but it will happen. A successful elk hunter plans for this. He knows that such a time will come and does not permit himself to be blindsided by it. He builds it into his plan for success. He will find ways to go beyond it. He will seek out others in camp and join with them to overcome these "blues." It is called discipline.

How can you mentally prepare for these challenges and adversity at elk camp? One way is to band together as brothers with your fellow hunters in camp. Building such relationships begins well ahead of Elk Camp. Such preparation is a yearlong effort. The Bible says, "A strand of three is not easily broken." I believe that we can learn a lot from this. In the context of Elk Camp it means that two are stronger than one and three are stronger than two. Get the point. Often, while Elk Camp may be made up of a group of guys (and maybe gals) who have something in common, i.e. elk hunting, they are really just a bunch of individuals in close proximity. Sometimes too close…whew. Just like a football or baseball team, the victory of the team and subsequent success of the individual players depends entirely upon the team's ability to focus upon a single objective and work together towards that objective. Now honestly, how many times have you seen that kind of teamwork in Elk Camp?

In our Elk Camp, we get together one or two times prior to camp to make a plan and get everyone all fired up. We also take an annual scouting pilgrimage to our hunting area in late summer. But one of the keys to our success is that we continually work on building our relationships with one another throughout the entire year. For us, Elk Camp is more like a getaway family reunion. Personally, I enjoy making Elk Camp enjoyable and memorable for the others a higher priority with each passing year. So what is the lesson here? One way to overcome the stress, strain, and blues is to commit to working together as a team to build one another up.

Huntin' Buddies

I cannot overemphasize the value of finding yourself a huntin' buddy. The following is a copy of a tribute that I wrote to one of my huntin' buddies, Rex Gardner. Rex was the truest of friends and closest of brothers. Some of the content of this tribute was originally written by another great huntin' buddy, Phil Weaver who granted me permission to include some of his thoughts here.

Good friends are hard to find. Good huntin' friends are even tougher. In the 33 years that I have been hunting, I have had the pleasure of being a field with dozens, perhaps hundreds of men of like mind, but I have only known three who I could truly call a "huntin' buddy." Three individuals in whom I have placed absolute trust, even to the point of my life year after year. This tribute is to my grand friend, mentor, brother in Christ, and most of all my huntin' buddy Angus (Rex) Gardner.

What is a hunting buddy? They are friends first, sons or daughters, husbands or wives or just someone you "bumped" into. Finding a good one is like "looking for a needle in a haystack", but when you do find one, you know it's for life. They are there with you when all others are gone, in good times and bad as well as the times in between when you just "need" someone, they are there willing to go the distance. They share in your victories and comfort you in defeat. When you take that bull of a lifetime, they are there. When you lose someone close to you, they are there. They share your passion. Be it the smell of fresh mountain air after a rain shower, or the cool mist of a foggy morning in the black timber. They also enjoy "just doing things" together. They are very hard to let go. But good times shared and memories will never fade and the promise of seeing them again keeps you going. To sum it up, if you have one, keep "um". "KEEPER'S ARE FOR LIFE."

Rex and I had been good, but occasional friends long before we discovered our mutual love for elk hunting and wild things. When I reflect on what most impressed me about my huntin buddy Rex Gardner, it was that he was chronologically old enough to be my dad and then some. During our trips a field over the years, he had the stamina, the drive, the enthusiasm, and the energy to be out of his bedroll frying bacon and scrambling eggs with Tabasco a half hour before my alarm would go off, when it was still darker than midnight and colder than you know where outside. With two bad knees, Rex could walk me into the ground nearly any day of the week during elk season. What passion, what love for the hunt, and God's creation could drive a man so…I can only imagine… and admire.

My huntin' buddy Rex remains not only my friend, but also my mentor. In our years of forging ice-crusted streams together, and climbing from basin to high mountain bowls to mountain peaks over and over again, Rex molded my character. By his example he taught me patience and perseverance, qualities that have proven to be essential not only to a successful hunt, but also to my life.

Elk hunting is hard work, anyone that says otherwise has either never been or has never really tried, but it offers rewards far beyond meat on the table to those who are willing to brave an unsure talus slope or scramble over the next ridge top. It was my huntin' buddy Rex who first showed me what waited for me on the other side of the pain one feels halfway up the mountainside. If you have ever hiked a few miles in the Rockies you know that this isn't flat land, and it ain't the going downhill that one remembers; it's those mind numbing uphill climbs that set your thighs on fire and cause you to think your lungs will burst, that God forever engraves in your remembrance. Yeah, it hurts some, but only for a short while. On the other side of the discomfort exists a cooling rivulet of clarity of mind and spirit that you may not have known even existed. Had my hunting buddy Rex not been willing to press on that extra mile and encourage me when I just wanted to quit, I would never have learned what lay beyond the next ridge.

Thank you Rex, you made a grand difference in my life. I thank God for you and the times we shared. As the truest of friends and huntin' buddies go, you're a keeper. I will always remember you, and if I don't see you again in this life, wait for me in the next. I'll be there when my day is through, and we'll go looking for wild things again.

I'll remember you forever, my friend.

It's An All Day Affair

I'm a firm believer in the fact that the more of ourselves that we invest in something, the higher the possibility for success in that particular endeavor. In the case of elk hunting, the hunter who works hard at it from before sunup to after sundown will have a distinct advantage over the hunter who takes a more relaxed approach. The differences between these two may be defined by what each hopes to get out of the hunt. If you are looking to have a good time, take it easy, see some great scenery, spend time around the fire, and in general kick back; there is absolutely nothing I can find wrong with that approach to a vacation. Just don't be surprised if the other fella who went at it hard, all day every day, comes back to camp asking you to help him drag his elk out of the woods.

Clearly this formula for success does not and cannot account for the "luck" factor. Luck is not predictable, but isn't it funny that the luckiest hunters seem to be those who spend more time working harder at it than those who do not?

Learn to Pace Yourself

Whether you are a marathon runner, a backpacker, or an elk hunter, those who participate in strenuous activities, especially in adverse environments like the high country requiring staying power, must learn to pace themselves both physically and mentally if they expect to finish well.

A second way to prepare mentally for the rigors of elk hunting is to break the day down into smaller, more manageable pieces. Like any sizable task, when approached head on in its entirety, it may seem to be overwhelming, or a far greater challenge that you can handle. So just break it up into a series of related events or actions that you can handle. For instance, a typical day elk hunting when broken down might look something like this:

- Arise early and hike to a pre-scouted observation point.
- Glass area and do some calling to locate bulls until one hour after sunrise.
- If no luck, move a mile and repeat, looking for sign and trails as you relocate.
- Repeat above approximately every hour until noon.
- Eat lunch or snack and reassess your plan. If no sign of elk or response to calling you may want to relocate to a different area. Always have alternative plans.
- Seek out bedding areas where elk hold up during the mid part of the day. Usually in dark timber.
- Begin glassing and calling sequence again and repeat, being sure to take short breaks, drink plenty of water, and eat high energy snacks.
- As the end of the day approaches, DO NOT start thinking about camp. This can be the best hunting time and you need to stay the course. Make a pact with your huntin' buddy to keep after them until after dark.

Obviously this is a very generic plan, but I hope you can see how I have broken the day into a series of separate events. Successful elk hunters know that endurance is key so they find ways to keep going when the going gets tough.

Avoid Getting Hung Up on Success, Enjoy the Journey

One sure fire way to ruin a great elk hunt is to tell your self, if I don't come home with a real wall hanger, the trip will have been a failure. Many of the best elk hunts that I have been on resulted in my coming home without any meat for the freezer. If you think that my situation is unique, it's not! I cannot tell you how many fellow hunters have said the exact same thing. A successful elk hunt will be exactly what you want it to be. You are the only person responsible for your personal expectations. If you set out to enjoy the experience from a big picture point of view, I believe that there is every reason that you will return home completely satisfied if you have done your homework.

On the other hand, given the ratio of bulls to cows in most public land hunting areas, and beyond that, the ratio of "trophy bulls" to cows being exceedingly low, i.e. maybe a 1:300 ratio of cows to bulls in the 300 B&C category. Your chances of nailing a trophy and fulfilling such a grand expectation is slim. Don't get me wrong, there are plenty of quality bulls to be found on public land, but the numbers are clearly not in the hunter's favor. The subject of expectations brings up another topic that I get to discuss with our readers at Colorado Elk Camp quite often. What constitutes a trophy animal? This issue comes up so often that I have chosen to devote an entire chapter later to this very subject.

One of my favorite expressions is, "Life is a Journey, Enjoy the Ride." Folks, I could (and may) write an entire book on this subject, but I will try to keep this discussion as brief and on topic as possible here. As a Christian and an elk hunter much of who I have become as hunter over the years has evolved from who I am as a person apart from Elk Camp. If I am honest and look back over hunts gone by, I have to admit that I am not always proud of the hunter that I remember from some of those times. I find it very difficult to understand anyone who can be one person 360 days a year and then do a Jekyll and Hyde routine and become someone else when they come to Elk Camp. I've seen it happen, but not often. My point here is that our experience as elk hunters is a direct result of the person we are when we are not in the field. What is important to me? How dedicated am I to the task? How do I relate to others? Am I an ethical hunter? The answer to these and many more are all questions that come from our daily lives, not rules for Elk Camp. The whole point here is that we cannot separate our elk hunting experiences from the rest of our lives. They are part and parcel. They are an integral part of the Journey.

As I write this, the big "FIVE 0" has recently passed me by and I find myself taking a good hard look at how I spent the first fifty years of my life. More so, I am pondering how I want to invest the next fifty years. If you have been here, you probably know what I am talking about, if not...your turn is coming. So

far the essence of my thoughts has led me to
the inescapable truth that our lives here on
earth are so very brief and time is precious.
When we come to the end of the final hunt,
we will not look back on the trophies, for they
will be long forgotten. We will look back on
the Journey. We will ask ourselves if we made
a difference in the lives of others, if we lived a
good life, and did we enjoy the ride. Try to
keep an eternal perspective and don't get hung
up on momentary successes, enjoy the
journey...make a difference!

Photo: 2 Chris Jeub's First Bull, 2001

Chapter 5

Big Country...
How to Keep From Getting
Lost

In the preceding chapter I mentioned that there was nothing that would ruin a great elk hunt faster than creating unrealistic expectations. Next in line of those items that often plays a significant role in a hunter coming home empty handed is the fear of getting lost. Granted there are not too many of us who will readily admit to this, but drop a guy who is unfamiliar with the territory off out in the middle of nowhere and see how far from camp he goes. Not only have I witnessed this phenomenon I have been that guy. There are all types of fears that we, as elk hunters, may be forced to deal with, but the fear of getting lost will surely put the skids on, keeping us from maximizing our potential for a successful elk hunt.

If you have spent much time reading what I have written over the years on Colorado Elk Camp, or for that matter, anyone who has written on this subject, you will see a common theme. If you want to become a more successful elk hunter, one essential ingredient in the success receipt is that you have to get away from the roads! I'll discuss this in greater depth later, but for now it is important to note that 80 percent of elk hunters will hunt within one mile of some type of road. The list of reasons for this self-imposed restriction is long, but having talked to many of these "road hunters," the fear of becoming lost in some very big country is at or near the top of their list. Consider this, if 80 percent of the hunters in any given area hunt within one mile of the road, how many elk do you think will be hanging out within that same one mile. This is a not rocket science folks. When we, the hunters, move into their territory, the elk will move out. So if you expect to find the elk, you will have to leave the roads and the pressure generated by the great orange hoards behind.

OK, so what can you do to help overcome any fear or concerns that you may have about your ability to find your way back to the truck, and at the same time manage to leave most, if not all of the road hunters behind?

First, there is no substitute for knowing the land that you plan to hunt like your own back yard. Unfortunately, even those of us who are fortunate enough to live in elk country do not always have enough time to maintain this level of familiarity. If your knowledge of the land is not at this level then it is very important that you have a good compass, a waterproof topographical map of your area and practical knowledge and experience on how to use both.

Let me take a moment to draw a special emphasis on the word "practical." How many fellow hunters have walked up to you and showed you their brand new $50 glow in the dark compass tied around their neck with some hand woven leather neck cord, and you knew good and well that they didn't have the faintest idea what to do with it? Unfortunately that is all too often the case.

Pardon me a minute while I wax on philosophically (it won't be the last time). These days many of us spend much of our time convincing others, usually in business but such behavior is far from limited to this arena that we know far more about a particular subject that we actually do. I know, I've been guilty of this sham on more than one occasion. Haven't we all? We may do this consciously or unconsciously, but we do it. After a while, this can get out of control and we can begin to believe in what are essentially lies about ourselves. I personally believe that all lies are wrong, you will have to make up your own mind, but wrong or not, some lies can and will get you into a heap of trouble. In the case above, the last thing a hunter can afford is to be way back in elk country depending upon gear or technology to help get him back to civilization that he has no idea how to use. While I guess it can be done, though I don't recommend it, learning to use your compass in the middle of a freezing cold moonless night, five or ten miles from a road with little or no clue where you are is, in my most humble opinion, way…way behind the power curve and just plain stupid.

Why not get ahead of the curve and take the time to enroll yourself in a short one or two day practical course in orienteering, better known as ground navigation. Groups such as the Boy Scouts®, Sierra Club®, NRA®, and other outdoor oriented groups offer these courses in most cities and towns throughout the year. Sporting goods retailers may also offer such courses, so give them a call. If they don't offer such a course, often the sales person can refer you to someone else who will know when and where a course will be offered.

In the event that you cannot find a ground navigation course near your home, a final resort is to purchase a book on the subject from your local bookstore or online from resources like Amazon.com. There are literally dozens, if not hundreds of good practical books on the subject, but one that I have found to be a good resource is, *Be Expert With Map & Compass, The Complete Orienteering Handbook*, revised and updated by Bjorn Kjellstrom, and published by Macmillan. ISBN 0-02-029265-1. The book retails in paperback for around $17.00.

GPS

Finally, there are few substitutes for a good personal GPS (Global Positioning System), a good supply of spare batteries, and a thorough understanding of how your GPS works. I personally use a Garmin eTrex Vista ®, because it has most of the features that I look for in a personal GPS and is very lightweight and compact. When I'm elk hunting, every ounce of additional weight counts because whatever it weighs in the morning will feel as if it has doubled by late afternoon. There are quite a few great GPS units out there, so shop around and find the one that best suits your personal needs and budget.

Though it took a while, GPS has finally come into its own. I remember not too long ago when if you told someone you had a GPS in your pocket, you may have gotten laughed out of elkcamp. Today, experience has shown that more hunters have them than not. They may not tell you about it, wanting you to think that their skills as a woodsman are more than they are, but there is a pretty good chance that somewhere in all that gear they are carrying around is a GPS.

Here is a great story to bear out the value of having a GPS with you in the backcountry. A few years ago, I was scouting some new elk country west of Rocky Mountain National Park. My partner (who shall remain nameless for reasons that will soon become obvious) and I had hiked a fair distance off the beaten path following some recent elk rubs, one rub leading to another, kind of like a trail of cookie crumbs. Well, we had been at this business of walking with our heads to the ground for some time when we decided it was getting late and time to head back to the truck. Our original plan had been to follow the rubs back out the same way we came in, only what we had not planned on was that the rubs were mostly on the opposite sides of the trees and were now pretty much invisible to us. Well, we wandered this way a bit and that way a bit, and before long, it became apparent to at least one of us that if we didn't get our act together, we could be spending a long cold night in the woods. After some deliberation, my partner pointing his finger said rather emphatically, "I think the truck is that way!" I wasn't quite so sure he was right, but on the other hand, I wasn't all that sure he was wrong either, when it hit me like a bolt of lightning. I remembered that I had put my brand new GPS, with the coordinates to the truck locked into its memory into my jacket pocket before we had headed out. So out comes the GPS, I click the GOTO window onto the truck coordinates and bingo, the course indicator says, "go that-a-way guys!" You would think it would end there wouldn't you? Not so fast. My partner's faith in that little gray box was less than what might be deemed enthusiastic. He didn't want any part of marching off into who knows where based upon some pie in the sky technology that he had never tried. So I said, I'm going this way (i.e. following the GPS.... due to training left over from my days of flying in the USAF. Sometimes you just have to trust your instruments). My partner says somewhat quizzically, I don't know? I say, tell you what, you go that way and I'll go this way, whereupon he saddled up and we followed the GPS bearing pointer directly to the tailgate of the truck. Soon thereafter, my partner went out and dropped a couple of bucks on his own GPS.

Features to look for in a good GPS:
- Easy to learn and easy to use
- Backlight feature for night use
- Relatively easy on batteries

- Altimeter feature
- Mapping feature
- Will accept software downloads from your mapping software.
- Screen large enough to see.
- Buttons work well with gloves on
- Tracks satellites somewhere more remote than when you are standing in the middle of a freeway, some older models will not.
- Affordable

Photo: 3 One of those elk rubs that we thought we could use to find our way back to the truck.

Topographical Maps

When it comes to having a security blanket out in the backcountry, for some it might be a difficult decision. Having a good waterproof topo map or a space blanket? For me, it's a no brainier. A good waterproof topo map can do both, keep you dry (somewhat) and help you to know where you are.

Maps that you can use for elk hunting come in a variety of sizes, scales, and levels of detail, depending upon their purpose and who produced the map. When you are planning your elk hunt, my recommendation, if you are unfamiliar with the territory is to go from big to small. That is, start with a map that covers a lot of territory in what I like to refer to as "the big picture" showing less detail such as a National Forest or Bureau of Land Management (BLM) map. These are typically scaled at 1:100,000. Both National Forest Maps and BLM maps are excellent for showing boundaries between public and private land, major land features such as rivers, roads, campgrounds, etc. BLM maps also include terrain contours as well, which can help to plan land navigation or identify benches where elk like to hold up during midday. Again, these are both a good place to start and can be purchased from their respective agencies and sometimes from your local map or bookstore.

Another good map that will often show more detail than either Forest Service (FS) or BLM maps are the Trails Illustrated™ series of maps produced by National

Geographic Maps. Not only are these maps made of a special waterproof and tear resistant material, but due to their approximate 1:40,000 scale, they show much greater detail with special emphasis on trails that may not be as apparent on FS or BLM maps. These maps are favored by backpackers and hikers and sold in many outdoor supply stores such as REI, EMS, and the like. Though they are a bit more expensive at around $9.00 each, they last nearly forever, and are updated much more regularly than FS, BLM or even USGS Topo maps.

This brings us to the map that I recommend that every elk hunter learn to use and have "with him" when he is afield in elk country, the USGS (United States Geological Survey) 7 ½ minute quadrangle topographical map. For purposes of this brief discussion, I'll just call this map a "Quad." Quads will by far show the elk hunter the greatest level of detail available in the area he plans to hunt. Roads, jeep and cattle trails, water sources such as rivers, streams and even swamps, vegetation boundaries i.e. general tree lines, meadows, and land contours are just a small amount of the valuable information that can be gleaned from a Quad. Elk are not fools and when they move from their nighttime feeding areas to their daytime bedding areas, they will typically follow the same or similar paths daily. These paths often follow particular contours of the ground to make the journey easier. A Quad can help the elk hunter identify probable travel routes long before he leaves home.

As the elk hunting season progresses, elk often change the elevation that they hold out in. A good elk tactic once you have located elk at a particular elevation, say for example

9,500 feet, is to draw a line along the 9,500-foot contour on your Quad and look for more elk along that same elevation level. Your Quad will not only show you the 9,500-foot line, but also help you plan your land navigation to other areas that may hold elk on that same line.

During the day, elk often will seek out cooler areas to bed down and digest the graze from the previous night. Many times the elk bedding areas can be found on benches or timbered areas of level ground located on the side of a larger slope or hill. Think of a bench as a small level notch taken out of a hillside. Sometimes these benches are only a few hundred yards across and nearly invisible to the naked eye. They can however in many cases, be identified and located using a Quad if you know what you are looking for. Let me tell you a personal story about hunting benches to illustrate this point.

It was around 1978. I was in the Air Force living in San Antonio, Texas and had gone on a mule deer hunt with a few of my neighbors to Southwestern New Mexico, east of Alamogordo. I was fairly new back then to the high country, and knew virtually nothing about mule deer hunting. My assumption, like so many, was that deer hunting was deer hunting, how different could it be?

Opening day of the season arrived and I headed out early like so many times in the past, hunting whitetails in Tennessee to look for a tree to climb up in and ambush some unsuspecting mulie. Most of you who hunt out west are probably falling out of your chairs laughing about now with this picture of some young whipper snapper from somewhere back east walking around the desert with his head

up in the air, or somewhere else, looking for a
tree limb to climb up in, in southern New
Mexico. Needless to say, in that particular area
of New Mexico tree limbs of any sort that will
hold a man's weight are few and far between
and had I done any amount of research on
where I was planning to hunt, I would have
known ahead of time that the land was
covered in Juniper and Pinion Pine.

    So like any newbie, I dropped off the
side of a road, walked down a few hundred
yards and sat down on a hillside overlooking
what appeared to be a "level notch" cut out of
the hillside. Is this starting to sound familiar? I
guess I had been sitting there glassing this way
and that, not really knowing what I was doing
for the better part of an hour, when I began to
hear what I thought to be the sound of
something slowly coming up the hillside from
below the "bench." The time was now, as near
as I can recall between 8:00 and 9:00 a.m. I was
facing west and the sun in the east had just
begun to clear the top of the ridge behind me
and started warming the bench below. As I
waited, rifle to my shoulder looking over the
top of my scope and feeling the pounding of
my heart in my chest like a jack hammer, a
beautiful four point (western count) mulie
buck stepped out of the Juniper on the west or
downhill side of the bench and began to slowly
graze his way across the bench completely
oblivious to my presence. What is important to
note here folks is that this little bench where
the buck was feeding and would likely have
bed down was no more than fifty yards across
and almost completely surrounded by Juniper
and Oak brush. It was not visible from above

or below, but would clearly show up on a Quad if one knows what to look for.

I wish I could make this story end with me coming out looking anything but a fool, but without some serious stretching of the truth I cannot. I was young, foolish, arrogant, and full of myself back then. For the better part of fifteen minutes, I watched that buck through my rifle scope graze that bench at a range well within 150 yards, a piece of cake shot. All the while, thinking in my arrogance and ignorance that something bigger and better would come along before the end of our five day hunt, I choose to pass and just said 'bang…bang'' as I watched the buck graze. Eventually, I think the buck winded me or just figured out something was not quite right, so he moved off. Ok, now you can really laugh!

The lesson here is that the buck had been down low feeding during the night and was on his way to bed down for the day. His stop on the bench could have been fortuitous for me. Perhaps he was planning to bed down on the bench, or maybe it was just a snack stop on the way to a nap. Either way, the bench presented the opportunity.

When I am planning a hunt, part of my pre-hunt research is to locate as many of these benches as I can find in my area. I then load them all into my GPS using the Latitude and Longitude coordinate extracted from my Quad, and then I plan a "stealth" route to each. This type of planning has many advantages, but one particular advantage that has proven itself of value over and over again is that by planning your route into and out of elk country ahead of time, you do not usually find yourself confronted unexpectedly by some river gorge a mile deep standing between where you are and where you want to be. Remember what I said earlier, *"Prior Planning Prevents…Poor Performance."*

Which Quads Do I Need?

First you will need to identify the area in which you plan to hunt. Then expand that by 20-25% to allow for the possibility that the elk may have moved to a nearby area for which you will want to have a map. Now you need to buy the quads that cover that area.

There are basically two ways to address the issue of buying quads for your area. One way is the way we have done it for years because there was no alternative. Go to the map store, sort through drawers and drawers of USGS Quads and hope that the ones you are looking for are in stock. Then take them home, lay them out on the floor and try to create a single usable map of your area by piecing all the separate quads together with tape. Now that you have them all assembled, you will have something akin to half your living room floor covered with this huge mosaic that will never make it out of the house, much less to elk camp.

There is however a much more simple, effective and cost saving solution, create your own custom designed and printed Quad!

Custom Topographical Maps from www.elkcamp.com

Colorado Elk Camp via our partnership with MyTopo.com® can provide you with custom printed waterproof topographical and aerial maps of your area for less than the retail cost of two USGS Quads from the map store. (See our ad in the back of this book)

To access this feature from the Colorado Elk Camp website just go to: http://www.elkcamp.com/Topo_Maps/topo_maps.html or click on the link to topo maps on our homepage: www.elkcamp.com.

There are lots of map products available, but Colorado Elk Camp and MyTopo.com specialize in producing maps that you design! Each waterproof Expedition Map and glossy Poster Map is custom-printed when you order. This unique system gives our maps some great advantages over other stock map products.

1. You can center your map anywhere
You precisely center your custom map anywhere in the lower 48 United States. This solves one of the biggest problems with stock maps... having to buy two, four, or more maps to cover the area you want.
2. Built to last
Our Expedition Maps are printed with waterproof and UV/fade-resistant inks on durable waterproof paper.
3. High detail and clarity
Every one of our maps is made from the most detailed USGS maps available. We print every map on special high-quality equipment to produce a beautiful, detailed map.
4. Personalized
Since you design every map, you can add your own titles, your name, and choose navigational grids for every map.

5. Fast
Finding the right map can be a hassle, but
when you design and buy your map from
Colorado Elk Camp via myTopo.com it will be
shipped quickly, usually within 24-48 hours.

A Special Request

While anyone can go directly to
mytopo.com and place an order for their map,
I would like to encourage you to place your
order through Colorado Elk Camp as the cost
is exactly the same to you, but Colorado Elk
Camp will receive a small contribution for each
map order that is placed via the links on the
Colorado Elk Camp website. This helps us to
continue building and maintaining the website
and making it an ongoing and valuable
resource to you and future elk hunters.

PC Mapping Software

When it comes to topo mapping
software for your PC, there are few products
available that can compare to Delorme's
TOPO USA.™ Granted that there are a host
of such software programs, but most are
limited to producing maps at scales no smaller
than 1:100,000. As I mentioned earlier in the
discussion on BLM and National Forest maps,
this scale is adequate for defining boundaries
between public and private land, and gaining a
general idea of the lay of the land, but you
really need a 1:24,000 scale to see how the land
really flows.

Some things to look for in a good mapping software include:

- 1:24,000 scale capability
- Route plotting
- Waypoints
- Map annotation capability
- 3-D Visualization
- Vertical profile projection
- Export to your GPS
- Import from your GPS
- High resolution print

If the cost of some of these software packages takes you back, keep in mind that in most cases you don't have to purchase the entire USA on a map. Many of these vendors sell their software broken down by region or even states. My software is regional, and therefore it cost me only a fraction of what the entire USA package would have. So before you go out and drop some really big bucks, do a little homework and see if you can find a product produced in regional or states versions. TOPO USA™ is such a product.

Chapter 6

Gearing Up For Elk

"Honey, I'm just going to run down to the sporting goods store for a minute. I won't be gone long." How many times does this phrase or something closely resembling it get repeated across America throughout the year? I'm not sure whether this is a "guy thing" or a hunter thing. Since I'm both, it is impossible for me to separate the two. I hope the women elk hunters out there will forgive my use of the male reference, but writing he/she is just far to confusing and time consuming. I don't know too many women elk hunters, come to think of it I don't know but one, but I'm sure that after writing this I will hear from a few. Back to the point, leave it to say that most elk hunters, that I've met are addicts to the activity, and along with the addiction of being an elk hunter comes an accompanying obsession to acquire new and better "stuff."

How much "stuff" is enough? Nearly thirty-five years of hunting tells me that for most hunters, there is no such thing as enough. There is always one more piece of gear that the elk hunter "needs." If you were to stop by my home and ask me to open the garage door, you would see what I mean. Front to back, left to right, floor to ceiling and in no particular order, almost every nook and cranny is filled, piled, or stacked with stuff that I use (or used) for elk hunting. Outfitter tents, camp stoves, boots, clothing, tarps, ropes, generators, the list goes on and on. Admittedly a lot of this stuff sits there in the garage and never moves, not even to elk camp, but you can be sure that at some point in the past, it was "necessary." Some folks are caught up in the accumulation of wealth; elk hunters are usually caught up in the accumulation of "stuff."

The focus of this book is "elk hunting," not elk camp, so my discussions on gear forego talking about what you need to have in camp and will be limited to stuff that will either help to keep you alive and comfortable during your time running around the boonies, or will help you to become a better or more successful elk hunter.

First, let me say that every manufacturer of elk stuff out there is going to tell you that in order to be a successful elk hunter you "have to have" this or that gadget. That's because it's their job, and if they want to keep their jobs and eat, they need to convince you to buy their "stuff." If you have an unlimited checking account and a warehouse of storage space, then by all means, knock yourself out, and go for it. Unfortunately, for most of us such is not the case. We must live on limited budgets, which means we need to use a moderate amount of wisdom and planning when it comes to making gear purchases. This may mean that we need to budget for that new elk rifle or bow and hold off until next year.

Case in point. Not too long ago, I was out with my great friend and hunting partner, Roger Medley helping him to look for a new bow. After driving to a number of sporting goods stores in the area and trying on a few, but not finding just the right bow, I asked him, what's wrong with the bow that you have? Before answering, he paused (which is his nature), then he gave me this, "you just let the air out of my sails", look and said, "nothing...I just want a new one."

Having deflated my friend, I determined to take the heat off and admitted that I too had recently been bitten by the gotta have it now bug. Due to a shoulder injury that required surgery, I had not even touched my bow in nearly three years, but I was "fixed" and wanted to get back into bow hunting. Like any self-respecting elk hunter, since my bow was almost new before the surgery, I said, I need some of those new carbon arrows. It's important to this discussion to note that I have nearly a dozen perfectly good, almost new, Easton X7® aluminum arrows loaded with never used Thunderheads™, but that didn't seem to matter. I wanted new stuff. But my talk with my friend had had its affect on me as well. Isn't it funny how that works? We lay these words of wisdom on others and it boomerangs back onto us? Anyway, it did, and I decided that I really didn't need any new arrows after all. Oh, by the way...Roger bought the new Parker Easy Draw®. He is a very happy camper!

Before I go on, let me make one more thing clear. Elk hunting is a sport, and as such should never come before your obligations and responsibilities to your family. The self-centered individual who consistently goes out and trashes the family budget with total disregard for the needs of his spouse and children will get no respect from me, and ranks somewhere below whale scum at the bottom of the ocean. Enough on that.

Like so many writers who have come before me as well as those that will follow, I realize that any discussion on hunting gear preferences is a receipt for trouble. No matter how hard one tries to be generic, open-minded, non-preferential, or whatever, someone out there is going to take issue with your point of view or opinion. So that having been said, keep in mind that the following is just that: one hunter's opinion or point of view. I will agree to respect that fact that you are entitled to yours if you will agree to do the same for me. OK, and then let's get on with it.

Choosing The Right Elk Rifle For You

At www.elkcamp.com I literally receive hundreds if not thousands of inquiries from hunters wanting my opinion on what is the best elk rifle. Why they think I have any more of a clue than anyone else continues to elude me, but never the less, they continue to ask. Well folks, for all of you who have been holding your breath, here is my answer. In my opinion, the absolute best rifle that you can have for elk hunting is the largest caliber rifle that you can consistently shoot the best. I had to toss that largest caliber thing in there because sure is shootin', some guy will ask if a .22 will suffice. No, a .22 will not suffice. In Colorado where I live and hunt, the Colorado Division of Wildlife stipulates that a legal elk rifle "must be .24 caliber (6mm) or more."

OK, now that we have excluded all the gopher whackers that leaves quite a range of boomers to choose from. In 2001, we took a poll of our readers at www.elkcamp.com on which rifle caliber was best for elk hunting. In the six months that we made the poll available, nearly 750 people responded with their opinion. Of those surveyed more than 80 percent argued that bigger was better, with either the 7MM Remington magnum or some version of the .300 Magnums being the rifle of choice.

As I get older, I find that I am less and less inclined to have to chase or track an elk for miles after the shot. My preference would be to have the brute's knees drop out from under him and plant him right there. Conventional thinking leads one to believe that if an elk is hit by a larger caliber round moving just below Warp 5, that he will stay put. Unfortunately, this is not always the case. Real life indicates that many elk when hit by very large caliber rounds like the 7MM Rem Mag, .300 Win Mag, .300 Ultra Mag, or .338 Mag. will still run off, sometimes as much as a mile before piling up.

There can be any number of reasons for this, but far and way, the #1 reason for elk not dropping to the ground at the point of bullet impact is poor shot placement on the part of the elk hunter. Accurate shot placement is the result of six things: 1) effectively tuning the rifle, round, scope, and shooter 2) Practice, 3) Familiarity with your setup, 4) Practice, 5) Practice, and finally 6) you guessed it. Practice. You can buy the best rifle available on the market, top it off with a $1,000 scope, load it up with custom hand loads and still end up chasing your elk all over the country or worse missing the shot if you do not take the time to become "one with the rifle." There is no substitute for getting to know your weapon, its capabilities, quirks, and limitations. I know a guy who recently went out and dropped around $1,000 on his new elk setup and was "surprised" to learn from me that the round would drop nearly 10 inches at 300 yards. His thinking was that this new round (lots of marketing publicity) and all the money he was spending might compensate for bullet drop and that bullet performance should be better. I guess it is better that he learned this at home rather than out in the field.

Tip#16: Know your rifle's performance capabilities cold!

Get into the trajectory charts and look up the particular round, i.e. 150 grain, 165 grain, 180 grain, for your caliber rifle and find out what you can expect it to do at 100, 200, and 300 yards. Then go to the range and validate this date with actual live fire. Keep in mind that you are looking for a caliber / round combination that will deliver a minimum of 1500 foot pounds of kinetic energy at impact. I used to think that the ability to shoot accurately while hunting was not that big a deal. Considering the kill zone on an elk is approximately 18 inches in diameter, I figured that as long as my range shooting at 200 yards kept all the holes inside a pie plate or approximately 10 inches, I had plenty of room to spare. Folks, this is a bunch of hogwash. When we are elk hunting, the elk can often move an inch, or a foot this way or that between the times we tell our brain to pull the trigger and the time the bullet can travel down range to the target. In addition my experience has taught me, and maybe yours is different, there is rarely a bench, sandbags, and stool around to give me a rock steady shooting position when I am ready to take the shot in the field. It should not take a rocket scientist to see where this argument is going. In order to provide for the highest probability of making an accurate and straight away lethal shot, we need to take as many of the variables out of the shooting equation as possible.

One of my good huntin' buddies, Phil Weaver (aka Ol'Arky) is the ultimate perfectionist when it comes to his shooting accuracy and consistency. Since Phil lives in Arkansas and I in Colorado, a lot of our communication occurs via telephone and email. Around mid summer, when Phil's shooting finger begins its annual twitching process in preparation for elk season which is still three or four months away, Phil begins what seems like daily trips to the rifle range to re-familiarize himself with his rifle. Phil is so meticulous about his shooting performance that I get emails regularly with Phil waxing on about why this new hand load that he has developed will not consistently hit within a 5/8-inch circle at 200 yards. 5/8ths of an inch! Phil, come on. Give the rest of us some slack!

Phil was, however, my mentor and motivation to become a more accurate and a more consistent shooter. It took some work and dedication to the task, but eventually I was able to compress my pie plate pattern down somewhat to hit consistently within a 1½-inch circle at 250 yards with my Remington 700 LSS in .300 Rem Ultra Mag.

Why go to such lengths? As I said earlier, elk hunting occurs in a dynamic and constantly changing environment. Factors such as weather, wind, moisture content in the air, altitude, one's nerves, shooting position, availability or lack of a rest, and finally target angle and movement are just a few of the variables that come into play for each shot that you may encounter. It is our responsibility as ethical hunters to prepare ourselves to perform at our best.

So far you may have noticed that I have avoided indicating any suggestions as to what are acceptable calibers for elk. Granted that over the centuries, thousands of elk may have been taken by the venerable Winchester ® 30-30-lever action. In my opinion, this round and the lower velocities and kinetic energy levels that it is capable of producing at the ranges that elk today are taken is stretching things about as far as they can go. Yes, you can take elk with a 30-30, but you better plan on being very, very close, or chasing him very, very far. My counsel is that whatever caliber rifle you choose, make sure that you and your rifle are capable of delivering a minimum of 1500 foot pounds of energy at impact. Some excellent readily available choices for elk rifles include: 30-06, 280 Rem Mag, 7MM Rem Mag., .300 Win Mag., .300 WSM, .300 Rem.

Ultra Mag., and .338 Mag. As you may notice this is a rather limited list and is based upon purely upon my personal experience. While there are lesser legal calibers available that are clearly capable of killing elk, these lighter calibers with their lighter weight bullets put even greater performance constraints on the elk hunter.

Bowhunting Gear for Elk

My years as a hunter began at the age of 14, bowhunting whitetails in western Tennessee, northeastern Arkansas, and Mississippi. My first bow had such a light draw weight, i.e. 34# that I doubt it would have done much damage to any deer beyond 20 yards. At the time, I didn't know that. Heck I didn't care. I was just happy to being hunting with my dad, Jim Houston, and brother Steve. Those were some really great times. Time together as a family, time together as men (boys), time together as hunters, that I will never forget. Sometimes I wonder if the reason I didn't see many deer in those days was that they were all down in some ravine laughing their heads off over the sight of that little bow and me.

Following that long ago time, I graduated to more powerful and more expensive recurve equipment like the Bear Kodiak Magnum and Super Kodiak, legends in their time. Today I shoot a single cam split limb Jennings BuckMaster compound.

Just the other day I was in a local Colorado Springs archery shop with my hunting partner, Roger Medley, who was shopping for his next bow. The owner of the shop was clarifying his opinion, which he is well known for expounding upon, on what makes for a well-balanced bow. Over the course of a hour, Roger and I learned a lot from this guy, who, according to himself, may be the single greatest wealth of practical archery knowledge in our area, opinionated or not. Among other things I discovered that he was not a fan of Bear Jennings bows. We also discovered that there is a lot of gear that he was not a fan of. I, however, love my *Buckmaster* and find that it is all the bow that I need. It may not be as light or have some of the newer bells and whistles that the latest higher tech bows have, but it does meet the # 1 criteria that the shop owner stipulated for what makes a good elk hunting bow. Similar to the criteria mentioned before in the discussion on elk rifles, what makes for the best bowhunting rig is one that you can shoot accurately and consistently.

Another valuable lesson that I have learned along the way regarding bow hunting gear is that one doesn't need to set your bow's draw weight to 70# or higher to be effective on elk. Elephants maybe, but for elk this may be stressing your back and shoulders more than necessary. This is again that "bigger is better" or "more is better" argument. In my opinion, if your setup fails the consistent and accurate test, bigger or faster is not going to make any difference. What does it matter if your arrow is moving at 300 feet per second or even the speed of light when it misses that bull that you've been stalking for three days?

Today, the state of the art in arrows is carbon fiber. Unlike their predecessor aluminum arrows, the major advantage of carbon arrows is that they will not bend. Having shot (and lost) aluminum arrows for over twenty years, carbon arrows were a welcomed relief to having to straighten or replace damaged aluminum arrows. Carbon arrows are also lighter and stronger grain for grain than aluminum. If you are considering the purchase of a new set of carbons, I strongly encourage you to avoid the off the shelf, shrink wrapped versions which may come close to matching the requirements of your bow, and just go down to your local archery shop and ask a professional to make you up a set specifically designed for you and your bow.

Boots.. Can Make or Break an Elk Hunt

Folks this will be the most brief and to the point discussion you find anywhere in this book. In my opinion, a well designed, quality built, waterproof, and well broken-in pair of boots is one of, if not the most essential item on the elk hunter's gear checklist. Nothing… I mean nothing will end a great elk hunt faster than having your feet go out on you because of poor planning in the footwear department. Becoming a successful elk hunter requires that you have the ability to go long and stay out long. This means having the capacity and gear to literally walk as much as ten to fifteen miles in unforgiving terrain every day. To do this day in and day out requires that you take good care of your feet and ankles.

I have heard the guys who say that they hunt in tennis shoes because they are comfortable and quiet. Folks, I just don't buy it. Why would anyone risk ruining an elk hunt for which they have waited all year or maybe a lifetime by blowing out an ankle or blistering up their feet just to be more comfortable or a bit sneaker in a pair of tennis shoes? A good pair of boots combined with some careful walking and planning will accomplish the same degree of comfort and quiet, while giving your feet and ankles the support and protection that they will need while hunting the ups and downs of elk country.

There are quite a few suppliers of quality hunting boots on the market, each carrying many models of boots. In all of my years of elk hunting, I have found Rocky Boots™ to be one of the best all around elk hunting boots available. Most of their hunting models are lined with GORE-TEX™, a waterproof material proven to be effective over many years. While there are other water-proofing materials, GORE-TEX™ seems to have become the standard for the industry. Another attribute of most Rocky Boots™ is that they do not require a break in period. I am on my second set of Rockies in five years (no the first set didn't wear out I just wanted some new Rockies) and I have never had to break them in. Just put them on, lace 'em up and head out like you have been wearing them all of your life. What more can you ask for? For my money folks, it's Rocky Boots! Keep in mind that not all good elk hunting boots come ready to hike in. Each model has its own set of attributes and you will have to do your homework. Just make sure that if your boots do require a break in period (most boots with a substantial amount of leather are in this category), you will need to get them into shape well ahead of hunting season, otherwise you may find yourself grounded after the first day of season because your feet have been destroyed.

Tip:#17 The bottom line here folks is don't go cheap on your boots.

Remember this. Everything you take into the field, your rifle or bow, your backpack, your camo gear, your food, your self, everything is piled on top of your boots.

Clothing

Next to a good pair of waterproof boots, a smart clothing plan for your day a field is critical for a successful elk hunt. Weather in elk country is finicky and it can and will change on you in a heartbeat. Just when you think you're prepared for a warm day during your early September bow hunt and head out of camp with nothing on but a light camo jacket, an unexpected upslope or Albuquerque low will blow in and whamo, you're five miles from the truck, snow is flying sideways, and the temperature may be dropping 10 degrees an hour. This is not good! If your clothing plan doesn't take the possibility of unanticipated weather into account, you could be in for some real trouble.

One of an elk hunter's greatest enemies when it comes to staying warm when in the field is moisture that can cause one's body heat to drop. I'm not a doc, but it doesn't take one to know that if your internal core body temperature starts to drop, it doesn't have to go far before hypothermia will begin to set in.

Hypothermia is defined as core body temperature lower than 95 degrees. When one's core temperature drops farther down to 90, you are considered to be in mild hypothermia. Symptoms are uncontrollable shivering. A person in this state of hypothermia will be pale and cool. They will exhibit varying degrees of confusion and incoherence, and experience trouble in making movements. Below 90 degrees, blood pressure, heart rate, and respiration decrease and the shivering reflex is gone. That's when hypothermia becomes really dangerous. Shivering creates heat, and once the shivering ceases there's nothing creating heat, you're just lying there, and your body is basically going to cool to ambient temperature and death is inevitable unless you get help.

A good strategy to deal with unpredictable weather while elk hunting is to dress in layers. This will allow you to strip off or put on more clothing throughout the day as temperatures or other weather factors may dictate. I usually hunt in mid to late October when temperatures are usually rather moderate. My layer plan is usually something like this: over basic underwear, I add a layer of wicking polypropylene long johns. Then I put on my pants and jacket, usually camo, with a wind blocker liner. I cannot tell you how many times I've sat on a hill side or ridgeline glassing opposite slopes for elk on a frosty October morning, and thanked God that He gave me the good sense to spend the extra money on the wind-stopper liner of my pants and shirt. I don't know why, but it seems as if that first hour after sunrise is far more windy and cold than sitting in the dark waiting for the sun to come up. The wind-stopper pants and shirt are followed by a jacket or parka lined with GORE-TEX™. Some folks prefer a waist length jacket. I have found that the extra length of a parka helps to prevent cold air from blowing up my back in those early morning hours when the wind is moving down the mountain against my back. If you've ever had a gust of cold artic air blow up the back of your waist- length-hunting jacket, you'll know what I mean. If the weather is pretty cold in the morning, I will also put on wool or a wool/polypropylene blend sweater over my shirt while planning to take it off and store it in my daypack as the day warms up.

A quick story here may help to reinforce the value of wearing good gear. It was opening day of Colorado's first 2001 elk season, and my hunting partner Mike Byrd and his son Josh and I had hiked for about an hour and a half to our pre-scouted spot for opening day. It had snowed somewhere between four and six inches during the night which had frozen over and made for a somewhat noisy walk as out boots cracked like breaking glass through the crust of snow with every step. Our spirits were high, as we knew the snow would help to move the elk. As we approached the patch of low-lying Juniper that we had planned to use as cover, a freezing North wind began to blow. Within what seemed to be minutes, the weather had gone from dead calm but cold, to freezing with 40 miles per hour snow and wind blowing sideways across us. Sitting on a bare mountainside above timberline with only those tiny ground-hugging Junipers to shield us from the wind, we must have been a pretty comical sight, as we tried to get out of the driving wind and snow. Mike and Josh were huddled up about a hundred yards north of me. I had unzipped the collar of my GORE-TEX parka and pulled out the stuffed hood and drawn it down tight over my watch cap leaving just enough open space over my nose to breathe. Then, I found a Juniper about sixteen inches high and did my best to get behind or underneath it, anywhere to get out of that hurricane of snow. I cannot recall ever being so thankful for having thought ahead and planned for such a remote possibility as I experienced on that cold and windy opening day.

There are many opinions as to what types of material constitute "the best" in hunting clothing, with wool being the predominant material of choice. The advantages of wearing wool are that wool will not only keep you warm in cold climates, but it also helps to wick moisture away from you when it rains or when your body warms up and starts to sweat. One major disadvantage of wool however is weight. Due to its density, wool products can be much heavier than some of its higher tech counterparts. From a personal note, I can't stand to have wool against my skin. The scratchin' drives me nuts. If you buy high quality wool clothing this will not be as much of an issue because the manufacturer know this and designs the garment with liners around sensitive areas like the neck, sleeves, and sometime liners for pant legs to prevent this very problem. So the lesson here is, if you are going to go for wool, do it right and don't go cheap.

Recently, industry has developed a fairly broad range of newer high tech fabrics that can provide high degrees of insulation without the associated weight or discomfort. Many of these have been adapted from other outdoor sports. The big advantages of some of these fabrics are lightweight and reduced volume. The down side of this is that as of this writing, few of these newer fabrics are available in camouflage patterns. But this is changing, so stand by. (I hope to be able to discuss these newer high tech options at greater length in my next book.)

It was not too long ago that if you wanted a quality cold weather jacket, goose down was your best choice. While down is an excellent insulator when dry, it takes up a lot of room in a daypack if your not wearing it, and provides absolutely no insulation when it becomes wet, which is very likely if you spend much time in the snow or rain while elk hunting. Needless to say, I avoid using down while hunting.

Finally, there is cotton. While cotton may be comfortable, it provides little insulation or protection from rain or snow, and when wet, it will take forever to dry. Unless you are hunting in warm climates with very little chance of getting wet, cotton is probably best reserved for sitting around the campfire.

Camouflage

The decision to wear or not to wear camouflage is again another one of those personal decisions. I prefer to wear camouflage whenever I am elk hunting or scouting for elk, as I am convinced that it provides me with a distinct advantage. For bowhunters, camo is an

absolute given the relatively close ranges of elk
encounters when bowhunting. Gun hunters
often argue that since most encounters with
elk during rifle season are at much longer
ranges, the argument for wearing camo is not
nearly as strong. That is fine if you can count
on the elk doing exactly what you plan on, i.e.
staying way out there at 200-300 yards. I don't
know what the experience of others is, but my
experience has convinced me that elk pretty
much do as they please, and will rarely if ever
do exactly what I want them to do. Therefore,
planning for a successful elk hunt requires that
we also plan for the eventuality of contacting
elk at close range regardless of what our
weapon of choice happens to be.

      The primary advantage of camouflage
is that is breaks up the outline of the hunter.
While eyesight is not the most powerful sense
of an elk, elk have over the years come to
recognize the upright shape of humans as a
clear sign of danger. The effective use of
camouflage will go a long way towards delaying
or even preventing the hunter from being
recognized as such.

      Camo is best used in conjunction with
sound elk hunting tactics such as using trees or
vegetation as a backdrop or stand. This allows
the camouflaged hunter to blend in with his
surroundings. Combine this with careful
monitoring of the wind, and a stand located
along a well traveled game trail and you have
the makeins' for a well thought out elk hunting
strategy.

      If you regularly hunt in the west and
wear camouflage, you will have realized like I
have that most of the major camo gear
designers, design their camo patterns for

Eastern hunting environments. These patterns frequently depict hardwoods, marsh grass, and dark barked trees with brown leaves. Unfortunately, while these do work to break up the hunter's outline, they don't do a particularly good job of blending in with the pines, aspen, and desert colors often found in western hunting environments. Many of these patterns often include photographically perfect representations that are indicative of hardwood forests. Unfortunately, high altitude western hunting in arid regions rarely if ever takes place in hardwood forests. The flora and fauna found in elk country is more likely to be represented by softer earth tones of tan, light green, and dark greens. A number of camo designers are starting to pick up on this need and designing their patterns to be less photo-realistic and more of a subtle blending of natural colors and shapes found in a particular region. A case in point is that a lot of elk hunting is done near or above timberline. Here a hunter is likely to have to position himself on bare tundra or even a rocky talus covered hillside because of the lack of vegetation at that elevation. In such a situation, wearing camo simulating a hardwood forest would stand out like a sore thumb. You might as well have a flag waving over your head.

A few years back on one of my bi-annual road trips to Cabela's (one of my favorite gear outfitters and places to hang out), I discovered that Cabela's had developed a new camo pattern called Outfitter Camo™. Outfitter Camo™ doesn't attempt to simulate any particular real world pattern. It is a subtle blending of light to mediums greens and a mousey gray color. The shapes of the patterns are similar to those found in military style BDUs, but larger. While I do have another set of camo for black timber hunting, I have found that my Outfitter Camo™ works very well in almost any western environment in which I hunt, whether it is hunting near or above timberline, aspen breaks, or dark timber. It has also proven to be a super pattern for spring turkey hunting.

GORE-TEX ™

Keeping dry while elk hunting is not only a matter of comfort it can be a matter of survival. As I discussed earlier, hypothermia is a very real threat in elk country and staying dry goes a long way towards avoiding its onset. While there are a number of waterproof or water repellant fabrics available on the market, GORE-TEX™ seems to hold the predominant position in the hunting clothing industry.

Early versions of GORE-TEX™ were stiff and noisy while walking in the woods, but current versions seem to have softened and quietened down considerably. I wear GORE-TEX™ lined boots, and a GORE-TEX™ lined set of camo gear in colder weather, and have been very happy with its performance. In addition to helping you stay dry, a GORE-TEX™ lining does a fairly good job at keeping the wind from passing through the garment as well.

Day Packs and Fanny Packs

Regardless of whether its hanging on your back from your shoulders or riding over your backside and hanging from your waist, you will need some method for carrying your gear around in elk country. Personal preference will again prevail but here are some points to ponder as you consider which choice is right for you.

Backpacks or daypacks as they are sometimes called come in all sorts of sizes, colors, and configurations. Some have external frames, while others have internal frames or no frame at all. With the exception of those made particularly for hunting, most daypacks are made from some type of nylon material. In my opinion, this is not the best choice for elk hunting. Why? First, synthetics such as nylon are hard and noisy and will make all sorts of noise as you crawl through brush in elk country. Second most of these come in bright colors, which are fine for your middle schooler to take with him or her to class, but stand out like a sore thumb.

A good elk hunting daypack should: 1) be quiet, 2) be large enough to carry your essential gear for the day but no so large as to allow you the freedom to haul more gear than you need, 3) be waterproof or at least water repellant, and finally 4) have a support system that distributes the weight evenly between your shoulders and your waist. If the daypack that you are considering does not provide some type of waist support, preferably padded, then you will be carrying the entire weight on your shoulders all day long. I can tell you from personal experience, this arrangement will wear you out in a hurry and may predispose you to leaving your gear back at camp the following day, which is neither a good nor smart idea.

Another alternative is the fanny pack. This arrangement carries your gear in a pouch or series of pouches on your waist, usually just above your backside. For those of us with little to no backside, the fanny pack doesn't always stay where it is supposed to unless one cinches it up so tight as to cut off circulation to the lower half of the body. Some new models come with a set of suspender type shoulder straps to prevent this downward travel. Qualifications for a good fanny pack are the same as those for a good daypack.

Recently some hunting gear manufacturers have come out with a third alternative, the big game hunting vest/pack. These have pockets and pouches all over the place to stow your gear. For the past two years I have been trying out just such a vest/pack and having tried everything else, I think I may have found a solution that works best for me. Using a vest type support system, my pack has numerous water repellant storage compartments, a compression storage area for holding a jacket, and a built in pouch and tube holder for a hydration system. This last feature is my favorite part as it allows me to carry 68 ounces of water supported by the entire weight of the system. The tube allows me to have the water right at my fingertips. No more canteens trying to pull my pants down. No more water bottles sloshing around in a pocket. No more excess motion when I want a drink. Just bite the tube tip opening the valve, drink, and I'm done. Another added plus is that as the water is depleted in the bladder, it collapses taking less room and preventing the water from sloshing around making unwanted noise. While I cannot find this exact same product anymore, as of this writing, Cabela's offers a very similar model called the Elite Scout Pack for about $69.95. See our list of essential daypack gear in the back of the book.

Optics

I cannot tell you how many times I have heard the following statement with which I wholeheartedly agree, "Don't go cheap on optics." This means buy the very best optics that your budget will allow. So many times I've seen or heard of elk hunters who have dropped anywhere from $500 to $2,500 on an new elk rifle and then top it off with a low end low quality scope.

If you have done any amount of research at all on rifle scopes you will have discovered that scope prices can run anywhere from your $39.95 discount store special to nearly $1,000 for ultra high end optics. I have always been a rather middle of the road sort of buyer, but my personal budget leans to the lower end of that middle point. I have therefore found a number of manufacturers that produce what I consider to be quality optics that will fit within my personal budget limitations of $200 - $300. Manufacturers like Bushnell, Burris, Simmons, Nikon, and Bauch and Lomb all produce quality optics in this price range. If your pocketbook can stand it, Leupold, Zeiss, and Swarovski produce excellent scopes as well.

When you are looking for a new quality riflescope a few attributes to consider are: Do you need a variable power scope or will a fixed power such as a 4x or 6x suffice? While I use an adjustable 4x-10x to help me identify the target at longer ranges, there can be a downside to the use of variable power scopes, that being that one can forget to crank it back down from its higher magnification setting before attempting to take a close range shot. A case in point occurred during a 2001, guided hunt with my friend Randy Horne, co-owner with his wife Jeanne of Bar-H Outfitters in Meeker, CO. During the course of a day's hunt, Randy's hunter had cranked his scope up to its maximum magnification for one reason or another and forgotten that he had left it on that setting, despite numerous "reminders" not to do so. Later in the day, the hunter was fortunate enough to find himself in the position to take a shot at a nice bull. When the hunter, having traveled clear across the country for this hunt of a lifetime and full of "bull fever" attempted to place the cross hairs on the bull. You guessed it; all the hunter saw was brown hair. Fearing that he would loose this opportunity he fired. The result was…you guessed it again…a missed shot at what was later determined to be roughly 20 paces. When the dust had settled, everyone was trying to figure out how he could have missed what should have been a no brainer shot at close range? A quick examination of the hunter's rifle answered the question. As suspected his variable power scope was again set to its maximum magnification. I wish I could have been there to see the look on both Randy and the hunter's faces. Randy is one of the easiest going friends that I have, but there are few things that will get an outfitter going more than discovering that one of his hunters is not holding up their end of the bargain, especially after they have been warned on several occasions. I guess the lesson learned here is, unless you are using a fixed power scope, make

sure that if your playing around with the
adjustable magnification feature, make sure
that you return it to a lower setting like 3x or
4x when you are done.

A second feature is the eye relief
distance for variable magnification scopes. I
am not the guru on this, I just know from my
own experience and that of others. When
some variable power scopes are in the proper
eye position for shooting and you adjust the
magnification setting from say 3x to a higher
magnification, you may have to readjust the
position of your eye (or the scope) either
towards or away from the rear of the scope to
keep the entire field of view in sight. From a
hunter's point of view this is really frustrating
and under the right circumstances could cause
a missed opportunity. Typically this problem
can be avoided by purchasing better optics.

A third factor to consider is that better
rifle optics are built from a single piece tube. It
doesn't take a rocket scientist to figure out that
the more pieces the tube is made of, the more
the chance of something inside become
misaligned. So stick with single piece tubes.
Enough said.

Finally, quality optics can significantly
reduce the amount of eyestrain that the user
will experience. I learned this lesson years ago
from a long time firearm expert, ex-Army
marksman and armorer. This same truth was
recently confirmed just recently by a call I
placed to a major optics manufacturer.

When the manufacturer of an optical
lens begins to grind a lens, he starts grinding
the lens at its center, grinding outward in an
ever-larger circular pattern similar to the
growth rings on a tree. In most cases, lower

priced optics will only have their lenses ground out from the center a small portion of the actual radius of the lens. When one's eye attempts to focus through this partially ground lens, the eye will try to focus not only on the clear ground area but on the opaque unground area as well, which can produce eye strain. As a rule, higher quality lenses have a higher proportion of the lens ground out to 100%, thus providing the viewer with a much clearer image and reducing the likelihood of eyestrain.

Try this test for yourself. Go to your local sporting goods optics distributor. The test works best with binoculars, as they are easier to view for a period of time. Ask the sales clerk to escort you outside with two pairs of binoculars, one in the $29.95 - $49.95 range and the other in the $150.00 - $$250.00 range. Try each pair out by holding it to your eyes for a minimum of one minute like you were glassing a far away hillside for elk. Now try the other pair, same deal. OK, compare the two as they pertain to the strain on your eyes. I've done this exercise many times and in every case, the higher quality set of optics wins out hands down when it comes to the amount of eyestrain experienced.

Tip #17: Don't go cheap on optics.

Chapter 7

Understanding Weather in Elk Country

Just last night I received a call from a guy living in Michigan, let's call him Bob. Bob is planning his first ever elk hunt to Colorado and like so many before was full of questions. As always, I was honored to take the call and help in any way that I could. I do this hundreds of times a year. Actually, such calls have played a large part in the motivation to write this book. During the course of what was about a one-hour phone conversation, Bob eventually got around to asking about how to plan for the weather for his upcoming hunt in Colorado. My response was to tell Bob that weather in Colorado during elk season, whether one is hunting in an early archery season or late rifle season, like the weather in nearly every other western state with an elk season, can change on the hunter is a heartbeat. To demonstrate just how diverse the weather can be I shared the following story with Bob.

It was late in the year 1990. I wish I could remember the month, but that sort of thing is to be expected once you pass 50. On this particular day I was washing my car out in the driveway and due to the unseasonably warm temperatures for that time of the year, I was enjoying the chore dressed in only some shorts and a tee shirt. About an hour later, I changed clothes and left for my job with the Air National Guard located about 60 miles south of my home. Here's the nugget folk. In two hours time and that 60 mile drive, the weather changed dramatically from a balmy sunny afternoon to a complete white-out with snow blowing sideways so strong that the two vehicles ahead of me drove off the road into a ditch because they could not see the road. Lucky for me I was in the rear of the column, or I would probably have been the first to end up in the ditch.

Tip #18: Plan for the weather to change for the worse, if it doesn't, so much the better.

While there may be any number of ways to plan for changes in weather, the following is my own personal strategy. Before leaving home, I pack two separate bags, one for warmer temperatures, and another for colder temperatures. Warmer temps can range from daytime highs in the 80s to lows in the upper 30s. Cold temps can bottom out in the sub zero range and may only reach daytime highs in the upper 30s. You need to be ready to deal with either case, especially if you've traveled some great distance across country for your hunt. This planning prepares me for nearly any eventually that may occur weather wise. Each bag will usually contain two sets of hunting clothing that I can put on and take off in layers.

Understanding the effects of weather in elk country can play a determining role in whether or not your elk hunt is successful. Anyone who spends much time in elk country will learn quickly that elk are attuned to the state of the weather. As mentioned earlier, the weather can change quickly and the elk will respond to these changes.

As a storm front begins to move in, elk typically will move out ahead of the front especially in late season. Late season is when the elk begin their annual migration from their summer ranges to winter ranges. I recall one late November day as I was driving back to Colorado Springs from Montrose when I came upon a line of elk, single file, stretched for nearly half a mile up a hillside. A small storm had blown through the night before and another large storm was forecast for the same area later that day. These elk were high tailing it out of there ahead of the storm along a major elk migration route. If a hunter knows these migration routes, he can use the weather to his advantage if he is patient.

When I was a newbie elk hunter I had a great time a field, calling elk, stalking elk, smelling elk, and dreaming of elk. The only problem was I rarely saw an elk. I was one of those guys who would come home year after year and tell friends that there were no elk in the area. I had hunted whitetail deer somewhat successfully most of my life, but this elk hunting gig was getting the best of me. When I look back at how I hunted elk in those years, i.e. no plan, no research, no foreknowledge of elk habits and habitat, no knowledge of the weather, the list goes on, I'm lucky I even saw one elk. Having grown up in the South, most of my foul weather hunting experience was limited to a little rain now and then. I had a very simple solution. When it rained, I went home. Unfortunately, this same habit had carried over to my elk hunting. Whenever the weather took a change for the worse, I packed up.

Photo: 4 Line of Elk Moving Out Ahead of A Storm

Tip #19: Guys...Wrong! Wait it out. While elk may hold up during a storm, they move like crazy afterwards.

Most storms make elk nervous. This can be for any number of reasons, but two are that with storms come winds, which reduce an elk's ability to hear, see, and smell danger. They are therefore on edge during the course of the storm and will often hold up in the timber until the storm passes. Once it has passed however, they are again on the move. The following story will help explain this.

It was Friday afternoon before the opener of the Colorado 2000 first limited rifle season and my hunting partners and I were out glassing a park where some of us intended to setup the following morning. We had been there about 15 minutes not having seen anything when the wind began to pick up from the southwest pretty quickly. I mean like one minute there is a gentle breeze and we were standing there comfortable in shirtsleeves, and five minutes later everyone was heading back to the truck and warmth. We all piled into Phil Weaver's Dodge and cranked up the heat waiting for the storm to pass. It was only a brief storm, but it carried with it some pretty good wind and corn snow. After about a half hour the storm passed and the sky began to clear again. As we were waiting, Phil says, "watch this. Keep your eyes on that patch of timber over there on the far western edge of the park." So like of bunch of vultures sitting on a tree limb, the rest of us tuned our radar to that spot wondering what Phil had seen. Someone says, "What did you see?" Phil says, "hush, be patient and watch." Sure enough, within minutes of the storms passage a line of elk, which eventually turned into a small herd of around 30 trickled out of the timber into the edge of the park to feed. Now most of us knew this, we just didn't take the time to think because we had got caught out in the storm with our pants down so to speak. All we had wanted to do was get out of the weather and warm up. Usually the bigger the storm, the more the elk will move afterwards. In the case of the example, the storm was small and the elk began moving almost immediately. Bigger storms may cause the elk to hold up for an entire day. The day following such a big storm may produce little elk activity but this is not the time to pack up and head out. Be patient wait them out. They will start moving again and probably with a lot more vigor than prior to the storm, especially if you are hunting late season and they are beginning their migration.

Tip #20: If you know how elk react to weather you can make it work for you rather than against you.

While I'm on the subject, let's talk about rain for just a moment. I hate rain! I've heard and agree with all the arguments that in our arid environment out West we need all the moisture that we can get to sustain habitat, and the economy, but it doesn't change the fact that I don't like rain. Growing up in the South, one comes to expect rain, mists, spring showers, or torrential down pours lasting for days. It is a way of life. I spent years moving from place to place just trying to get away from it. For me there is just nothing good about being out in weather and getting soaked. Here in Colorado, rain is rare, especially during elk seasons, but it does occur if the temperature stays warm enough. Elk respond to rain of any kind in a similar manner as they do to the storms mentioned above. They hold up. Rain coming through the timber is noisy and reduces an elk's ability to hear. This reduced ability to detect danger will make elk really skittish. It can however work to the hunter's advantage if used properly. The smart elk hunter will use the noise of the rain to cover his own noise while hunting the black timber where the elk tend to hold up in such times. Keep in mind that the elk will be on red alert, but if you move slowly, watching the wind, and

Tip #21: Keep a keen eye for movement of some patch of color that appears out of place or a horizontal line like the back of an elk existing where horizontal lines should not appear you might get lucky.

The Wind

This brings us to the wind. There is probably no other single environmental factor affecting the potential outcome of an elk hunt more underrated than the wind. The smart elk hunter knows that the wind can be his greatest asset or his worst enemy, and he factors its affect, its presence, and its direction into his total elk hunting strategy.

An elk's sense of smell is its primary detection mechanism against danger. It is important to keep in mind that the wind in elk country is constantly changing and the smart elk hunter knows this and is always alert and prepared for the change. One of the worst feelings while elk hunting, though sometimes unavoidable, is to make a long stalk on a nice bull only to feel the coolness of a breeze hit the back of your neck as you are about to settle down and take the shot.

Tip #22: A general rule to keep in mind while elk hunting is to hunt uphill in the

early morning hours and downhill in the latter morning and afternoon.

This will allow the hunter to take full advantage of the wind caused by the natural heating and cooling of the earth's surface. In the early morning hours cooler air will flow down slope because it is heavier and there is little warm air below rising to resist it. Once the sun comes out and the earth's surface begins to warm, the ground heats up and a convection effect begins to take place where the air near the surface warms and begins to rise. Eventually, on most days, this rising effect of the warmer air will overcome the weight of the higher cooler air and cause the wind to shift and begin moving up the mountain. The successful elk hunter will plan on this and ensure that the wind is in his face as opposed to on the back of his neck.

It's important to keep in mind that this up slope/down slope convention is a general description of daily wind movement. It does not take into account the fact that wind is strongly affected by geography. By this I mean that things such as canyons, mountains, ridgelines, and other geographical features all affect the speed and direction of the wind, causing it to continually change direction. Altitude can also affect wind direction and speed. In general, the higher one goes, the fewer obstructions there are to interfere with the passage of the wind. As one approaches timberline or crosses over a ridgeline, you may experience the wind surging from a gentle breeze to strong gusts. Wind direction may also change, sometimes as much as 180 degrees from what you may have experienced at a lower elevation. The smart elk hunter is always on the alert for any change in the wind, no matter how small.

Here are a few tips that may help you to keep track of the wind. Try tying a small six to eight inch piece of sewing thread to the end of your bow or rifle. Anytime you need to check the wind's direction, just hold your bow or rifle up in the wind. The thread will always blow downwind. If the elk are in the same general direction as the thread is pointing, it is time for you to move. In such a case, especially if the elk are close, it doesn't matter whether you go left or right, just move to get the wind off of your back.

Another tried and tested method for keeping track of wind direction and speed is to carry a small squeeze bottle of "unscented" white talc. Both the bottle and the talc can usually be found in your local drugstore. Talc is very light in weight and carries well on the wind. For a wind check, just gentle squeeze a small amount of the talc from the bottle into the air and note which direction it travels. Again, as with the thread, the talc will drift downwind or with the wind. If it comes back at you or moves left or right and you think the elk are in front of you, from a wind perspective, everything is cool...for the moment. Remember, wind direction can change at any moment. I can see a question forming in the minds of many who may read this. How much or how often should I be doing these wind checks. I guess my best answer is that you are out there to hunt elk, not be a weatherman. If you return to camp at the end of the day and a full bottle of talc is empty, then you are spending way too much time and energy checking the wind. Learn to look for other signs of wind movement such as the way trees may be bending in the wind, or the direction that the grass in a meadow is bending. These are subtle, yet very significant clues that a smart elk hunter learns to pick up on. Once you attune yourself to the natural environment around you, you won't even need the talc.

Tip #23: Make sure that if you use talc, it is the "unscented" version.

Squirting a bunch of foo-foo smelling stuff into the air will not produce the results that you had expected, but it may get you a kiss from some lovesick cow elk.

Another way to determine wind direction is to watch the elk. In most circumstances, when elk bed down they will usually lay down with their noses into the wind. If you're glassing a herd of elk on a hillside, look to see which way most of them are facing. That is the probably the direction from which the wind is blowing. For example, say you are looking north and see a herd of elk lying on a slope across a draw from you and most of the elk are facing to your right. That means that the wind is likely coming from the east. Since you don't want to plan your stalk to approach the elk from upwind, consider taking a circular approach to the west (your left) and coming around the elk from downwind. This gives you a higher probability of your scent not making it to the elk and spooking them into the next county.

Like humans, elk have to work at staying warm as the temperatures drop. While their hides do a much better job of insulating than our skin, it is still a matter of survival for the elk. When the wind speed picks up, the elk are often forced into the timber to break the force and effect of the wind. This has a number of affects. First, it makes hunting more difficult because a hunter's movement in timber is harder than movement in the open. A hunter climbing over deadfall and through underbrush is much less at home than the elk. The hunter's chances of seeing elk before the elk see him in black timber are significantly reduced. Additionally, the elk are on edge in such a situation because the noise created by the wind interferes with their ability to hear and thereby detect danger.

Chapter 8

Calling All Elk

If there is a topic of discussion related to elk hunting that is more openly debated than the value of calling elk, I haven't heard it. I, for one, am a strong advocate of the sensible (emphasis on sensible) use of elk calls, especially cow calls.

I've got to tell you one my favorite stories about this subject. It was sometime back in the early '90s and I was hunting alone in the Gunnison area of Colorado. I was set up just below the crest of a ridgeline overlooking a couple of well-used game trails. About 50 yards beyond the trails was an old grown over Forest Service fire road. I guess I had been in place for about an hour or so, when I hear a cow calling from somewhere up the forest road to my left. So like any good elk hunter, I whip out my trusty cow call and answer her back. Sure enough back she answers. This conversation goes on for a few minutes and I can tell that the cow is moving closer and closer. Finally I decide it's time to shut up and see what happens rather then run the risk of getting busted. Well, this cow starts calling and calling and calling, like every five seconds, like she doesn't have a friend in the world. I mean literally! Listening to this cacophony, it starts to dawn on me that something may not be right, or at least not as it seems. For the next couple of minutes all I hear is this cow, or what I had thought was a cow going off over and over. About that time, the mystery becomes clear as two hunters on horseback come riding down that Forest Service road still hootin' like crazy on those cow calls...both of 'em! It must have taken these guys another five minutes to pass out of my range of hearing, but for all that time, they just kept hootin' on those cow calls. Since that time, I have had the opportunity to listen to many elk, singles, small herds, and large herds. By comparison, the only amount of cow talk that has ever come close to the amount of racket that those two hunters were making as they rode through the woods that day, has been the cow talk of medium to large herds of elk in the early summer when the calves are about and elk talk is everywhere. I guess my point here is that if you are going to use an elk call, it is important that you know how to use it, and more importantly when to use it.

Bugling vs. Cow Calls

Many agree that the days of bugling in big bulls, while not extinct are definitely on the decline. Over the years, the more mature bulls have learned not to trust the sounds that they once may have taken for those made by their own. Not being an elk, I don't know what they think of them; all I see is how they react, which is usually to move off in the other direction. This is not a hard and fast rule, and I'm not saying that you should chuck your grunt tubes, but evidence and experience by far more hunters than myself suggest that outside of the rut, bulls are loosing interest and responding less and less to these types of calls.

It would appear that major distributors of elk calls are also seeing this decline. As evidence of this, next time you visit your local sporting goods retailer, take a look at how much shelf space is given to cow calls as compared to the space dedicated to bugles and grunt tubes. Just the other day, my hunting partner and I were in one of the newer and larger sporting goods retail stores here in Colorado Springs looking for turkey calls, which just happen to be on the same wall as the elk calls. Clearly cow calls claimed a far more significant amount of shelf space. In addition, while the cow calls were located in prime space placed at eye height, the grunt tubes were laying flat on the bottom rack nearly out of sight. Retailing is about moving gear, and gear that sells gets a higher priority on the shelf than gear that does not sell as well. What does this story tell us? Maybe it tells us that more and more elk hunters are choosing to use cow calls today.

OK, all that being said, bugles can be used effectively during the rut, especially the early part, to help the elk hunter locate elk. During the rut, with all those elkmones (hormones) raging, bulls will tend to throw caution and good sense learned over years to the wind. During the early stages of the rut, the bulls are in the process of establishing territory and gathering cows to breed. When they hear another bull screaming (this is you), often times they will respond in kind to tell you to "stay away, this is my land...get outta here or there is gonna be a fight!" Responses like this can be used by the smart hunter to know where the bull is and help plan a strategy of approach.

Once the rut gets into full swing and the bulls are "cowed up" meaning they have established their harem, their life becomes a full time, 24 hour per day, routine consisting of breeding, keeping their cows close, feeding (when they have a spare minute) and running off lesser bulls. All of this requires tremendous amount of energy and time when they can least afford to use it as they are preparing to go into winter. This in many cases predisposes the bull to flight rather than fight when challenged by another bull (your bugle). I have seen countless examples of bulls moving their cows quickly into the timber at the first sign of some unseen intruder (some hunter's bugle) during mid to late rut. Don't get me wrong here. If another (real) bull shows up, and you see it, get ready, there is a better than average chance that there is going to be a fight.

Types of Cow Calls

There are basically two types of cow calls, the mouth call or diaphragm, and the reed call. Both types have proven to be extremely effective in almost every elk-hunting situation; the basic difference being the amount of time it takes the novice to learn use the call.

In my opinion, the mouth call or diaphragm is the better choice for a number of reasons: 1) Once in place in the mouth, it doesn't require any external body motion to use it. Your hands can remain still and are free to hold onto your bow or rifle. This may not seem to be such a big deal to the rifle hunter who expects to encounter elk at long range, but for the bow hunter who must get in close for the shot, it can get a little tricky holding a bow with one hand, drawing with another, and attempting to hold onto a reed type call at the same time. In such situations, diaphragms are clearly superior. 2) Diaphragms are capable of producing what most veteran callers agree is a clearer and smoother reproduction of those sounds actually produced by cow and calf elk. 3) Diaphragms can be used in conjunction with grunt tubes to extend the range of the call or even help to redirect the sound of the call. This last part is important. When an elk hears a call, like humans, it will attempt to determine not only who is calling but also from where they are calling. If the hunter is directing his call straight towards the elk, the elk are going to be able to zone in on the hunter, which may not always be a good thing. By using a mouth call in conjunction with a grunt tube, the smart elk hunter can redirect the sound of the call by bending the tube to the side or rearwards, thereby causing the sound to appear to the elk to have come from somewhere other than the hunter's position. This head fake often causes the elk to come in on the hunter's right or left making for a broadside shot rather than a difficult head on shot.

The only downside to using a mouth call is learning to use it. Unlike reed type calls, which are almost fool proof, diaphragms do require a bit of practice and some getting used to. Because diaphragms fit into the roof of one's mouth, some folks find that there is a tendency to gag, which is a normal reaction to something large and foreign in the mouth. When I was first learning to use a mouth call, I had this same problem. Some folks are prone to this reflex action, while others never notice it.

Tip #24: The key that I found to overcoming the gag reflex was to place the call in the side of my mouth outside of my teeth.

It didn't seem to make any difference if it was in the upper half of my mouth or the lower half, all that mattered was that because it was there, my brain began to adjust to the presence of this foreign object in my mouth. The longer I left it there, the less I thought about it. The less I thought about it, the less the gag reflex. After a few minutes, I found that I was able to move the call into place with my tongue at the front part of my pallet. From time to time, early on, the gag reflex may come back. If it does, move the call back to the side of your mouth. Don't take it out all the way unless you think that you are going to swallow it. The longer you can leave the call in your mouth, the quicker you will adjust and can then begin to use the call.

My focus in *Elk Hunting 101* is not to teach you how to use a call, but to help you make some informed decisions on your options of which calls to use. I'll go into greater detail on how to use particular elk calls in our next volume *Elk Hunting 201.*

Reed type calls are a great alternative to the mouth call for the new elk hunter. These calls are mostly barrel type calls with a mouthpiece on the front end of the barrel and a plastic or other synthetic reed inserted into the mouthpiece. The caller simply inserts the mouthpiece about ¼ inch into his mouth, bites down gently and blows. This action causes air to move over the surface of the reed, which then vibrates and produces a sound that is amplified through the barrel. The caller controls pitch and volume by the pressure on the bite (less pressure equals lower sounds, more bite pressure equals higher tones) and the amount of air pressure blowing through the call.

Reed calls are very easy to learn to use. I use an *Ace-1* ™ cow call from Sceery. It sells for around $22.95 and can be purchased with an instructional tape at most suppliers. I've used many other cow calls and still do, but for the beginner, the *Sceery Ace-1* ™ is tough to beat.

One of the best ways to learn to use either type of call is to purchase a CD or cassette tape of elk calls available from most suppliers and then mimic the calls on the tape with your call.

Tip #25: Where you accomplish all this practice is entirely up to you, but experience has taught many of us who have been there not to try this in the house. Unless you are one of the fortunate few who has a very…very understanding spouse when it comes to disturbing the peace in the home, you may want to do

this in the car or truck on the way to or from work.

When to Call and When to Hush

Remember the line in the old song *"you've got to know when to hold 'em, know when to fold 'em."* Folks, if you want to be successful at calling elk, a similar rule applies, you need to know when to call and you need to know when to be quiet. Elk are not all that different from us in the way they communicate with each other. Human communication is a two-way affair. If you say something to me or ask me a question, it provokes a response, or for each action there is a reaction. If you start talking to me and I fail to respond, you may determine that I've lost interest and you will probably stop talking. Elk behave similarly. Unless there are outside influences, they may carry on conversations throughout the day as long as someone is talking back, whether it is another cow, their calf, or someone who sounds like another elk. My rule of thumb is, once I have established a conversation, keep talking, keep the conversation going, and keep the interest level up until the elk begins to move so close as to be able to distinguish that you are not the real deal. How close is close can depend on factors such as cover, terrain, weather, wind, etc. Factors that would extend or reduce the elk's ability to detect the sound that they believe to be a real elk, and determine that it is really you.

Like talking to another human, suggestive calling tends to work better than aggressive calling. There are exceptions to this rule, i.e. calling bulls during the rut, but over all persuasion appears to work better. If you are working a bull that is all fired up during the rut, you may want to try to sound more aggressive, more threatening. Some bulls will respond in kind and come charging towards the call attempting to drive off a potential threat. On the other hand, he may gather up his harem and hightail it right outta there. Aggressive calling is always risky, but may be the only way to lure the bull your way. If you do manage to bring in one of these monsters, be ready! This is especially true for bowhunters who must wait until they almost can see the whites, or in some cases red, of the bull's eyes before taking a shot. In such cases, I might think about having a large tree handy that I could get behind, if that bad boy gets too close.

A case in point can been seen in one of my friend Wayne Carlton's videos where Wayne is out shooting some video tape and finds himself on one side of a rather small tree with 800 pounds of really angry, red eyed, snot blowing bull elk lunging on the other side at what appears to be a range of about ten feet. You might want to ask Wayne what was going through his mind as he experienced this "close encounter of the elk kind."

Finally, a smart elk hunter knows when to be quiet. As mentioned above, once the elk is in close or you think that he may have located you, it's time to hush, get ready, and keep your eyes open to any kind of movement. Remember the earlier story of the two guys on horseback hootin' and hootin' on their cow calls? While elk do talk considerably throughout the day, the same elk doesn't talk every second. Just like humans, too much talk

can have an adverse reaction with elk as well.
Communication whether with people or elk is
a balance of listening and responding. If you
are ever fortunate enough to find yourself
within hearing range of a herd of elk, take the
time to listen to them for a while. I've done
this many times, but my focus is usually on the
hunting or learning to imitate the sounds of
their talk. By listening to the conversations, we
can learn not only the sounds, but we can learn
how the dialog plays out, the nuance of the
communication process, even if we cannot
understand it. If there are a lot of cows and
calves there will surely be a lot of conversation,
but not all from the same elk.

**Tip #26: Cow calling should resemble a
persuasive conversation, not a contest to
see who can talk the most or the loudest.
It's about building a relationship. Think
about talking to your wife. Which works
best gentle persuasion or yelling? I think
that most of you will get the point. Enough
said!**

Chapter 9

Proven Methods of Elk Hunting

As I have said before, elk country is "big country," and to be successful in your hunt requires one to develop tactics and strategies that may be different from those that you have used in the past while hunting woodlots or pastures for whitetail in the Midwest or back East. Since elk, for the most part, travel in herds; the successful elk hunter needs to be prepared to cover as much territory as possible during the course of his hunt. This requires a plan. I grew up hunting whitetail in the South. The tactic there was to climb up in a tree and wait there, for the entire season if necessary, until the deer came within gun or bow range. This tactic is very successful due to the dense deer populations in the South and the fact that whitetail travel as singles or small groups, thus spreading them out over a wide area. Ok, so now you know the difference between the way that elk travel and the way that deer travel. So how does one hunt these monster deer-like critters called elk?

Run and Gun...

Sometimes known as Spot and Stalk, this tactic requires the hunter to identify a number of prominent or high spots from which he can glass with binoculars a fairly large piece of real estate. This might be a ridge fingertip, a clear-cut, a south facing hillside, or a rock outcropping overlooking a draw. Any position that gives you the ability to visually inspect a large tract of land will do.

Because of the great line of sight distances that may be involved in this process, i.e. anywhere from a few hundred yards to perhaps miles, it is important that the smart elk hunter bring with him a bucket load of patience. Now you may be saying to yourself, patience...me? Who is this guy kidding? I cannot even spell patience much less maintain any. Remember the old cartoon of two vultures sitting on a limb and one says to the other, "Patience heck, I want to kill something." Guys, you can! When it comes to sitting and waiting, I am the least patient person I know. At the grocery store, if the lines are too long, I'm the guy who will just put it back on the shelf and come back another time rather than wait in line. But when it comes to elk hunting and all the time, effort, and expense that I have put into a hunt over the course of a year, I learn to practice patience...at least for a week. If I can do it...you can do it.

How long do I stay in one spot before moving on to the next?

Tip #27: The answer here is, as long as it takes for you to glass absolutely every single inch of ground that can be seen with your binoculars or 'Mark One' eyeball.

That could be a lot of glassing you say. You bet it is. Think of it this way. That trophy bull you are seeking is hiding out there somewhere, maybe bedded down behind that lone Juniper, perhaps standing facing away from you just on the edge of that clear-cut. He is the pot of gold at the end of the rainbow, and the reason that you are here. Why would you shortcut your pursuit because you get tired of looking? Elk hunting is NOT convenient, and it's NOT easy or for the faint of heart. If it were, the statistics showing an average success ratio of 1:8 (one successful elk hunt every eight years) would not hold true. If you want to score every time you go out, go shoot some tin cans. When you are glassing, you will need to look for parts of the elk. It is not often that you will see an entire bull or cow elk standing out there broadside like a magazine cover with a sign nearby saying shoot here. No, most elk spotted in this manner are located by the smart elk hunter training his eye to notice things that appear out of the ordinary like the horizontal line of an elk's back when nature produces mostly vertical lines. Or it could be a momentary glint of sunlight bouncing off of an antler, or the tan patch of an elk's backside against the backdrop of green timber. Look for parts, movement, anything that will give you a clue as to the presence of the elk. Believe me, this is not easy. We have all read the magazines and watched the videos or cable channel and images of full size elk are branded on our mind's eye. It is only natural, that when we go looking for elk, that we look for the entire beast. This takes some work and focus, but you can do it.

Once you are sure that you have glassed the entire area, you might even consider doing it again. During the early morning and late evening hours, elk are constantly on the move; either to or from bedding areas, and in this travel they may move through the area that you are glassing. While you are glassing, consider using your call. You will be surprised how far the sound of a bugle or cow call will carry from such an unobstructed point, especially if used in conjunction with a grunt tube to direct or amplify the effect of the call. Many successful elk hunters can attest to the fact that this is a great way to locate elk.

If after thoroughly glassing an area and trying your call a few times in the process, you have not seen any elk or had any replies to your call, it is time to pick up your gear and head on to the next similar spot that you determined before heading in that day. Remember…always have some type of plan for the day. This allows you to effectively cover the most ground in the least amount of time and precludes the possibility of you just wandering around elk country in circles. Use your topo map and compass or GPS to help you move from point to point.

OK, what if you do see that 6x6 bull or hear cows talking from my lofty perch, what do you do now? Folks, here is the point where you have to get smart and commit…the stalk. Here is where you need to reach way down inside to that hunter- gatherer embedded deep within your DNA and come alive. It's right now that you need to take into account all the factors that may affect the outcome of your stalk.

Factor One - Wind: The first is the wind. While your high school geometry teacher may have taught you that the shortest distance between two points (you and the elk) is a straight line, there is a better than average chance that this straight line isn't going to work for your stalk, but you would be surprised how many times I've seen hunters do just that. Like a bull in a china closet, they see or hear a bull and like a race horse coming out of the gates, they are on the move heading directly for the critter with little, if any, thought or consideration to the effects of the wind.

An elk's sense of smell is its #1 defense against a predator and like it or not, folks that's exactly what we as elk hunters are…predators. One whiff of an elk hunter, whether it be the bacon and eggs that you ate for breakfast stinking up your gear, or that bar of soap that you washed off with last night, it doesn't smell right to the elk and they will be outta there like a shot if they wind you. Before beginning your stalk you need to develop a plan taking the wind into account. If this means, and it does more often than not, that you will have to plan a circuitous (that's a circle) route around the elk to approach them from a more favorable wind direction, then that is what you have to do.

Factor Two - Geography: Many times this type of a stalk will require you to walk much farther than a direct approach would have, including covering some pretty nasty terrain, this is where your level of commitment will be measured.

Factor Three – Commitment:

Tip #28: The deciding factor in your success at this point will be the answer to two and only two questions: How bad do I want this? What am I willing to do make it happen?

I hope that you would have asked and answered these questions before you left home, but many times the real test of commitment that can lead to a successful elk hunt comes right here. It is time to fish or cut bait. Are you in or out? Sure you are…made the decision…I am ready. I will do it…this is why I am here.

While you are making your stalk, it helps to keep in mind that wind changes all the time in elk country, especially in canyons where it can swirl all over the place. Use your wind checker (mentioned earlier) regularly as you proceed to make sure that you either stay downwind of the elk or you have some type of terrain between you and the elk to keep your scent from reaching them if a portion of your stalk requires that you be upwind for a time.

Tip #29: As a rule, it is usually better to approach elk from above, i.e. uphill of the elk.

This is true for a number of reasons especially if you are hunting during the middle hours of the day. First, during late morning and mid day the heating of the earth forces the warm air to rise and move from lower elevation to higher elevations or up hill. Second, when elk bed on hillsides they tend to orient themselves facing downhill or into the wind. Finally, it is my experience that more often than not, when shot at, elk tend to run uphill. This last tip is not a guarantee, just an observation, so don't go running off and telling your hunting buddies that elk will always run uphill when shot at. As sure as you do, you or someone is going to miss a shot and that elk is going to run straight downhill and you will have some explaining to do.

Stand Hunting

Stand hunting in elk country is usually limited to hunting over water holes or wallows. Wallows can be anything from a spring, to a seep, or even a small pond like body of water. Elk frequent these for water and also to help cool their bodies. Wallows vary in size from just a few feet in diameter to as much as twenty feet or so across. Some may be filled with muddy water (a good sign that it is in use), while others may only hold the mud. Frequently used wallows will show plenty of elk sign in the way of tracks, muddy water, and trails leading into and out of the area. Heavily frequented wallows are excellent locations for setting up a stand.

Stand hunting over wallows can require even more patience that the run and gun approach as it requires the hunter to sit very still and quiet for long periods of time. When selecting your stand over a wallow here are a couple of factors to consider: 1) Clear shooting lanes – the smart elk hunter will position his stand to give himself a number of unobstructed directions of fire as it is difficult to predict from which direction the elk will approach the wallow. The key here is to give your self as much flexibility as possible. 2) Wind – the smart elk hunter will do his best to determine the prevailing wind direction near the wallow and factor this into his plan to keep his scent from drifting toward the wallow or the approaches the elk might choose to use it. Ok, you ask, what if there are trails leading to the wallow from all directions? Try to determine which trail or trails are being used the most and focus on these. There are no guarantees that you will pick the right one, just use your best judgment. Some hunters are using those little game cameras that they place near a wallow to snap photos of the game automatically as it comes in. If your checkbook can handle it, these tools can provide clues as to who is using the wallow and how they approach it.

3) Cover – the smart elk hunter will use natural cover to his advantage. Since wallows are often found in smaller clearings surrounded by timber as opposed to out in the middle of a meadow, there is a good chance that the hunter's encounter with the elk will be at close range. Movement or sounds that may go unnoticed by the elk at long range will almost always light their afterburners from close range. When hunting from a stand, I recommend the use of good camouflage including a head mask so that your form and minor movements will appear to the elk as just another part of the landscape.

Ultimately, the success of your elk hunt will be affected by many factors. Whether you choose the run and gun method, stand hunting over a wallow, or combination thereof is up to you and the movement of the elk in your area. Whichever method you choose to use, have a plan and execute the plan.

Chapter 10

Outfitters: Good Ones, Bad Ones and Maximizing Your Elk Hunting Investment

For those who do not have the luxury of living in elk country like I do, or the financial and time resources to travel back and forth regularly to scout the area that they plan to hunt, the options for planning a successful elk hunt become rather limited. Other than just heading out into the boonies with little or no information, which I would strongly discourage for about a hundred different reasons, the serious hunter is left with one viable option. Hire an outfitter.

For those who choose this option, there are basically three types of hunts available: the fully guided hunt, the drop camp hunt, and the trespass hunt. Let's take a brief look at each of these to see how they differ, what you can expect, and how much each may whack your wallet, which, more often than not, is the deciding factor.

The Fully Guided Hunt

A fully guided elk hunt is the crème-de-la-crème the once-in-a-lifetime elk hunt. The average fully guided hunt in Colorado (2004 prices) will set you back between $3,000 and $3,500 per hunter. When you book a fully guided elk hunt, you can expect to hunt with an experienced guide who will know the country, have good knowledge of where to find elk, and have the ability to put you and probably one other hunter (normal guide to hunter ratio is 2 hunters per guide) in position to harvest a legal animal. If your guide is able to place you in a position for a shot, that is considered by most in the industry to be a successful hunt. Contrary to popular belief, a successful hunt is not defined as one where the hunter actually harvests an animal. Factors that can prevent this are: the hunter can't shoot worth a flip and misses the shot, the hunter gets too nervous and blows the shot, the hunter says something like "that bull is not big enough." All these are factors controlled by whom? That's right, by the hunter, not the guide. If you are looking to harvest a certain (minimum) size bull, say 300 or better, then that is information that you need to discuss with your outfitter before you sign the contract. Reputable guides will tell you right off the bat if the area that they are licensed to hunt can provide you with a reasonable chance of harvesting such a bull.

Tip #30: Keep in mind however, that regardless of what anyone tells you and what historical success ratios they can produce, NO ONE can or should guarantee that you will be able to harvest any animal, much less a particular size trophy.

Granted that many areas and ranches manage herds that may offer significantly higher opportunities for larger animals, but nothing is guaranteed in a "fair chase" hunt. Let me clarify what I mean briefly by fair chase. Fair chase means that the elk are free to roam anywhere! There are no restrictions on their movement, there are no high fences, and there is no bait or artificial or man-made inducement for the elk to remain in a particular area.

Additionally, on a fully guided hunt you can reasonably expect the outfitter to provide you with other services such as a comfortable base camp from which to hunt complete with heated sleeping quarters, which can range from a lodge or cabin to a heated tent. You can also expect the outfitter to provide you with quality nourishing meals during your stay in elk camp. Often times these meals are provided by a camp cook whose sole responsibility is to take care of your eating requirements. Make sure that you are clear about what type of meal to expect. If you have special dietary needs, these are your responsibility to bring to the attention of the outfitter beforehand. Many a hunter has gone home grouchy or disappointed because he paid big bucks for a hunt and didn't get steak and lobster for dinner every night. Make sure you understand what you are buying. By the way, if you do find an outfitter serving steak and lobster, would you let me know!

Finally, on a fully guided hunt you can expect the outfitter to provided you with transportation for you, your gear, and your game. This means horses, ATV's, or some form of motorized transportation from the trailhead to camp. If your outfitter says that you must transport yourself and your gear to camp, I would take a very close look at exactly what else was not included in the deal. This being said, there are camps, mostly from some type of lodge or permanent camp that you can drive to in your own vehicle. This is, however, usually the exception. You can also expect the outfitter or guide to pack the carcass out from the kill site. Depending upon your contract, you may or may not have to prepare the animal for transport yourself. This means you may be responsible for field dressing the animal. If this is the case and you are not capable of field dressing the animal, you will need to discuss this ahead of time with your outfitter. In most cases, however, they will take care of this work.

The Drop Camp Hunt

Drop Camp hunts are basically a modified and less expensive version of the fully guided hunt. A typical drop camp hunt in Colorado will run between $1,100 and $1,500 per hunter (2004 rates). The outfitter typically provides all the same services and accommodations as above with the exception of the guide, food and field dressing services. Your outfitter will deliver you, your food, and your gear to a preset camp located in good elk country. He will give you and your group some pointers about where to hunt, and he will come back to check in with you from time to time (typically every other day) to see if you have game down that needs to be transported to storage. Basically, however, once the outfitter leaves camp, you are on your own. In some situations, the outfitter may even maintain contact with your camp via two-way radio or cellular phone if such service is available.

Drop camp hunting is advisable for those on limited budgets who are experienced hunters and are physically prepared for the rigors of high country hunting. In most drop camps, horses are not left in the camp with the hunters. There are exceptions to this rule, however, where the outfitter will rent horses to you for an additional fee. Horse rental fees can average $150 per animal per day, plus the cost of feed.

Tip #31: Something to keep in mind here folks, maintaining stock on an elk hunt is a lot of extra work and you can expect this to add a minimum of two hours to your already long day, every day.

That is, if everything goes just right. If the horses get loose during the night, it is your job to find them. If they get sick, it is your job to care for them. If they get cranky, and they will, it is your job to deal with it. Most packhorses run anywhere from 3 to 12 years in age. So think of it like this. It will be like taking a 1,200-pound child or adolescent along for your hunt. Also, it is important to keep in mind that horses are not like pickup trucks. You cannot just park them and expect them to be ready to go when you walk back up to them. If you are not well experienced with handling stock, I suggest you forego them altogether.

A final option is that you may be able to make an arrangement with the outfitter to leave a wrangler in your camp during the course of the hunt. His sole responsibility will be the care of the stock. You can expect to be responsible for feeding him, as well. This service almost always comes with an additional fee that can average $150 per day extra just for the wrangler.

The Trespass Hunt

Trespass hunts are basically self managed hunts on private property. In return for a fee, which can average $1,000 - $1,500 per hunter in Colorado (2004 rates), you are given the keys to the ranch, maybe a few pointers and camping rules, and the blessing of the outfitter or landowner to have a great time. In most cases, you and your group will have the exclusive use of the property for the duration of your hunt. This should be stipulated in the contract. I suggest that it is always a good idea to have a written contract even on a trespass hunt. It helps to keep everyone honest and defines exactly what is being purchased. There have been recent cases where hunters pay a fee to an outfitter or landowner for a private land hunt only to find out too late that the private land or ranch is a small forty acre parcel that backs up to public lands like a national forest. In such a case, the hunter has dropped some serious bucks for the privilege to walk across 40 acres to hunt land that he could have hunted for free. Be smart. Know exactly what you are buying into.

Trespass hunts can be a very affordable way to hunt private land without the cost of land ownership. Why would one want to hunt private land? In some cases, once the season begins and the pressure from so many hunters builds on an elk herd that lives mostly on public land, the elk will have learned that by crossing over onto private land, they are safer. If you are the fortunate hunter who has contracted to hunt that particular ranch, lucky you! Another advantage of hunting private land is that you can avoid having to hunt with so many other hunters stationed behind every tree and rock. Private land hunts are truly an experience worth the investment if you want to get away from the "orange hordes".

Good Outfitters, Bad Outfitters…& Knowing How to Tell the Difference

In 2004, there were approximately 775 outfitters here in Colorado registered with the State of Colorado Department of Regulatory Agencies (source: DORA). While there are no official records of non-registered outfitters, reliable sources suggest that there may as many as 300 individuals acting as outfitters that have no state registration, may have no insurance, may have no first-aid training, and may have no experience whatsoever acting in the capacity of an outfitter. Believe it or not, I have personally talked with people who wanted me to broker hunts for them who considered themselves outfitters based upon one criteria, they either owned or managed a piece of property. Can you believe it?

Let's talk about what constitutes a good outfitter? First, let me qualify the following with the fact that this is my opinion. I know, everybody has one and few want to hear it. Well, it's my book, so you get my opinion. If you choose not to agree, that's fine. There are six major attributes that I believe must be evident to constitute a good outfitter.

1. Integrity
2. Knowledge of land, elk, hunting strategies, and people
3. Experience on the ground with real people hunting real elk
4. Registered with the state regulatory agency for outfitters
5. Verifiable references
6. Quality Guides and Gear

<u>Integrity:</u> Integrity means that an outfitter and all those who work for him or her are people in whom you can place your trust. They are straight shooters who are going to tell you God's absolute truth whether you want to hear it or not. They will only promise to deliver that which they can reasonably expect to deliver. They do not "stretch" a story to make it more appealing. They will back up whatever they say with action and are not afraid to be held accountable for their promises or actions. They respect the land and their actions are always within the law and regulations of the regulatory agencies appointed over them and the land that they are licensed to use. Registered outfitters are required (in Colorado) to provide you with a contract of services. The language

in this contract is stipulated and gives a clear definition of those services that the outfitter is going to provide and what you as a hunter can reasonable expect in return for your check.

<u>Knowledge:</u> A good outfitter will have a thorough working understanding of: 1) The land whether it be private land, National Forest, or BLM land, 2) The elk...their travel patterns and their escape routes, 3) A broad variety of hunting techniques including spot and stalk, still hunting, and stand hunting, 4) People skills...this is critical as the last thing you need is some outfitter chewing your head off because he doesn't like you, 5) Camp management, 6) Business practices, and 7) The abilities of his guides and his stock just to round out the list. Here is a quick perspective on the people skills issue. I recently heard the story of an outfitter who is reputed to have fired a gun at the feet of one of his hunters (like in the movies) because the hunter said something the outfitter didn't like. Now I cannot verify the truth of this, but it did come from a very reliable and knowledgeable source. These are the guys that give legitimate outfitters a bad name and, in my opinion, might need to spend some time in a very small room as a guest of the government for a while. <u>Experience:</u> All the book knowledge in the world cannot make one a good outfitter if the knowledge has yet to be taken to the field and tested and refined on the land. Books are great, but experience is the true measure of what works and what doesn't in a particular situation.

Registered: The difference between a registered and an unregistered outfitter boils down to one issue, accountability. The registered outfitter recognizes his or her responsibilities and duties to the hunter, the state, and the public in general, and is willing for someone else to hold them accountable. The unlicensed outfitter doesn't really care about any of the above. He or she is only interested in his or her own welfare. He has little regard for the law, the public, or the hunter.

Verifiable References: If an outfitter is reputable, he or she will be more than willing to grant ready access to references of both good and bad hunting experiences. In addition, in the state of Colorado, DORA (Department of Regulatory Agencies) maintains a database of complaints and sanctions against any registered outfitter as well as actions taken against unregistered outfitters. This information is available on their website: http://www.dora.state.co.us/outfitters

Quality Gear and Guides: A good outfitter doesn't go cheap. He delivers a quality hunting experience for a fair and competitive price, and does not make excuses. His gear including accommodations, sleeping arrangements, stock, tack, and camp equipment are serviceable, healthy, and in good repair. His guides know the land, the elk, their travel habits, their feeding and bedding locations, and where their water sources are. They are in good physical shape capable of hunting from dawn till dark. If hunting from horses or mules, they are well trained in the management and handling of the animals and know how to minimize the potential of an accident for themselves and their hunters. They have excellent people skills and know when and how to tell a hunter "no." As hunters, we must realize that it is not only the guide's responsibility to provide us with the best hunting experience that he can, but he is also responsible for our welfare and safety. If that means that he needs to draw the line to keep us safe, then he needs to have the skills to do that.

If you are trying to choose an outfitter and are concerned about how to go about picking a good one, run them up against the list above. Do all the research on the one that you like the best, and then ask yourself if the deal seems fair. If it sounds too good to be true, it probably is and maybe you best keep on looking.

Sometimes a picture is worth a thousand words. The following story from a good friend is a word picture of what can and will go wrong if we don't do our homework when choosing an outfitter.

Often times when Easterners head out West, our heads are dancing with dreams of what we think elk hunting really is. We may have a good idea of what elk are and what hunting them is like, but something that is foreign to many of us is that we don't always know what to expect from an outfitter. This is especially true if you have never had the privilege of hunting with a guide.

Although I am an experienced hunter, finding a good outfitter can be hard and often times there are just as many bad as good. On a recent trip to Colorado, I searched for weeks before I made the final decision on an outfitter to hunt with. Why did I choose this guide? He said all the right things. He knew what to tell me to convince me that he was a first class and reputable outfit, but was crafty enough not to tell too much. I was told we would have Class-A accommodations. I was told I would be into elk every day. I was told I would be hunting with experienced guides. I was told I would have a 90% chance of getting a shot. I ate this up like a kid in a candy store. Unfortunately, Class A accommodations turned out to be a pop-up camper with a propane heater, and we never saw an elk. Needless to say, we never got a shot and from my point of view our guides didn't have any experience guiding bowhunters.

Looking back on it now, I could have done a few things to stop this from happening, but I didn't and I learned the hard way. My advice to all readers is as follows:

1. Get every little detail in writing. For me this was hard thing to do. Reputable outfitters will have a contract that states everything that is expected of both the outfitter and the hunter. By getting everything in writing, you ensure that if things go bad and the outfitter does not hold up his end of the bargain, you have some ground to stand on.

2. Checking references is good, but often times the only people on that list are the outfitters' friends and his high paying clients who have had the red carpet rolled out for them for years. You will rarely see hunters who went home empty handed and were dissatisfied on that list. Your best resources for choosing a guide are friends you can trust who have been on successful guided hunts or a

hunting consultant. A friend will not hold back on telling you the good, bad, and the ugly. Another method is to use a hunting consultant like Jay Houston of Colorado Elk Camp. A good consultant carefully researches the outfitters he uses and has learned over time what hard questions to ask of a new outfitter.

Elk hunting is just that - hunting, and even if you do not see elk, you want to have a good time. Any well run operation will try their hardest to put you on elk, and if that is not possible, they will at least show you a good time and give you lasting memories.

Just remember one thing when talking to outfitters that is also true in life: If it sounds too good to be true, it usually is. If your gut feeling tells you a certain outfitter is trying to pull the wool over your eyes, cross him of the list!!!

God Bless,
Tracy Breen
God's Great Outdoors Magazine Editor

Chapter 11

What's a Trophy Elk?

This answer is so easy. I could make this the shortest chapter in history, but given that the whole concept of *Elk Hunting 101* is to provide you with some basic tools to become a more successful and smarter elk hunter, I'll elaborate for a while.

I get hundreds, if not thousands, of contacts (I don't count them) every year from elk hunters or wannabe elk hunters asking about trophy elk. Comments like, "I want to hunt trophy elk," or "what units are the best for hunting trophy bulls?" or one of my favorites, "what is the ratio of trophy bulls to regular bulls and cows in area (whatever)?" I get these because Colorado Elk Camp is a recognized online resource for providing elk hunting consulting services via my website, www.elkcamp.com.

The best answer that I can give you to the question of what is a trophy is this. A trophy elk is whatever you consider a trophy to be. The rest of the world has many different methods for measuring trophy status, but the rest of the world is not you. If you are looking to get into the record books, then there are some very specific guidelines as to what constitutes a trophy class bull. The Pope and Young Club® (archery) minimum score for a Yellowstone Elk to enter the books is 260. The Boone and Crocket Club® (firearm) uses a minimum score of 360 for typical American elk for entry into their record book.

Over the years, hunters have come out of the woods with elk of all shapes and sizes. Some bring out the monsters that you see on the covers of magazines and videos while most bring out younger 4x4s and 5x5s that might score in the low to mid 200s, and let's not forget the hunter who is in it for the meat and chooses to harvest a cow. One thing that almost all of these have in common however, regardless of the size of their "trophy" is the big ol' grin on their faces when all is said and done. Few are the hunters coming out of the woods complaining that the bull or cow that they took was too small. Those that do whine like this usually find themselves hunting alone, if at all, the following season.

Chapter 12

Bringing It All Together

Elk hunting is one of the toughest, yet most rewarding North American big game challenges the hunter can experience. It can, however, be one of the most frustrating. As I have tried to communicate throughout this book, the difference between the highs of reward and lows of frustration is to a great extent dependant on two factors: the level of planning or preparation that you put into your hunt, and the personal level of commitment of each individual to do what it takes to become a successful elk hunter. Essentially, if you want to become a successful elk hunter you can, but you have to get smart.

My goal in writing this book was to give you an overview of the elk hunting experience, to impart some measure of knowledge that you may not have had already, to reaffirm that knowledge that you do have, and to leave you with some tips on how to become more successful in your future elk hunting adventures. If I have managed to do this to any extent, then I will consider this effort a success. I remember when I first moved to Colorado and started elk hunting, it was like trying to break into some good ol' boy's club. Nobody wanted to share the wealth of information available to help a fellow hunter learn. I made a pledge right then, that if I ever figured this "elk hunting" thing out, I would share it with whoever wanted to learn. That is why I created Colorado Elk Camp and it has also been the motivation for writing this book for you.

If you want to learn more about elk hunting, stand by for our next volume in this three part series, *Elk Hunting 201 ©*. While *Elk Hunting 101* is designed to be a very basic level course, *Elk Hunting 201* will begin to delve into some of the more technical aspects of the sport. In *Elk Hunting 201*, we will focus on the "how to" aspect. In addition, there will be in depth discussions on new entries into the arena of outdoor gear that can be used for elk hunting that you may not find in the "hunting" department. Have you ever found yourself five miles from the truck with a ton (heavy) of gear that you wish you hadn't brought along because of weight or bulk. In *Elk Hunting 201* we will be offering you some alternative solutions to this problem by helping you to think outside of the box.

We will also go into detail on specific tactics that have proven to be successful for hunting elk, some old and some new. Are you comfortable finding your way around in elk country? If not, we will help you to learn some basic rules for land navigation. Finally,

Elk Hunting 201 © will be full of Tips, just like *Elk Hunting 101*. If you are very forward thinking, keep in mind that our plan is for this series to be a three volume set, so hang in there for *Elk Hunting 301 ©* as well. I don't have any idea what this volume will include, but you can be assured that it will be packed with insightful information, informing experiences, a bit of wit and humor, and more of the great adventure we call Elk Hunting. If you have an idea on a topic that you would like to see investigated and discussed in *Elk Hunting 301*, let me hear from you via our email address at Colorado Elk Camp, elkmaster@elkcamp.com

Safe Hunting and God Bless,
Jay Houston

An Elk Hunter's Essential Gear Checklist

The following is a list of basic yet essential gear for the elk hunter to take with him on the hunt. When I first started hunting elk here in Colorado I was a proponent of the 'More is Better' theory. What I learned the hard way was that the more I took with me the more my back hurt at the end of the day. Today many years (and miles) later I have adopted what I believe to be a much smarter approach, i.e. 'Less is More.' Translated, this means the less gear I haul out on my back in the morning, the less my back hurts and the longer I am able to hunt.

- Daypack or Fanny pack with water container (bladder types with hose and mouthpiece work best)
- Global Positioning System (GPS) and Compass
- Topographical map (waterproof)
- Flashlight (small like Maglite™)
- 2-Way radio (if legal in your area)
- Extra batteries (all electrical equip.)
- Sharp knife & sharpening stone/steel
- Cow call(s)
- High Carbohydrate Energy food (Bars, Trail Mix, Drink, etc.)
- Space blanket (a good one)
- Sunscreen (SPF 30+)
- Bug repellant (seasonal)
- Flagging tape (1/3 role-fluorescent)
- Rain Gear or Poncho (Lt. Weight)
- First Aid Kit (small, incl. moleskin)
- Matches (or lighter) & Fire starter

ABOUT THE AUTHOR

A life-long hunter and outdoorsman, Jay Houston began his big game hunting adventure bowhunting whitetail deer with his dad and brother in the Oak and Hickory hardwood forests of western Tennessee, Arkansas and northern Mississippi. In 1969, Jay made his first hunting pilgrimage west to Rifle, Colorado where he became forever captivated with the Aspen covered Rockies, and broad open spaces he now calls home and refers to as "Elk Country."

Jay is the President of Colorado Elk Camp, www.elkcamp.com, an online resource he founded in 1996 to provide information and services for elk hunters and outdoor enthusiasts. Serving nearly four million visitors a year, Colorado Elk Camp has become one of America's leading purveyors of information for elk hunters. When asked why he started Colorado Elk Camp, Jay says, "When I first moved to Colorado and started elk hunting in 1989, there were few places one could go to obtain information on elk hunting and fewer hunters willing to share some of the most basic information essential to learning about this great wilderness adventure. I determined that if I ever broke the code and learned anything of value to other hunters, that I would find a way to share that information."

For over a decade, Jay has hunted elk throughout Colorado and served as a hunting consultant helping thousands of elk hunters to locate just the right outfitter or elk hunting ranch to meet their particular hunting needs.

As a freelance writer for over 20 years, Jay has authored and published numerous articles and stories on a wide variety of topics. An interview on Jay's thoughts on elk hunting can be found in a comprehensive article on elk hunting published by Heartland USA™ magazine November/December 2003 issue). Elk Hunting 101 is his first published work in book form.

About The Photographer

Jerry Taylor, who shot our cover photo and most of the elk photos in this book, has lived in the Rocky Mountain West nearly all of his life, with most of his years spent on the northern Colorado Front Range. He has also lived in southwest Montana, as well as four years in the Badlands of South Dakota.

Jerry is an independent professional photographer specializing in wildlife, nature and scenics. He is also an accomplished portrait, commercial and wedding photographer. His wildlife and nature photos come primarily from the great sweep of the Rockies and their surrounding plains, ranging from southern Colorado and Utah through Wyoming, South Dakota, Montana, Alberta, British Columbia, and Alaska.

Not content to roam the backcountry with a camera only, he is a life-long hunter and a member of the Rocky Mountain Elk Foundation and the NRA. Each year's elk camp with his close family is his passion. He also hunts deer, moose (when he can draw a license), upland and small game, and waterfowl. Jerry will even sneak off to remote trout streams, high country lakes (both frozen and not), and occasionally to northern Saskatchewan, always searching for the perfect fly or lure or just a great sunset, usually accompanied by his wife and best friend Lori. Jerry can be reached or copies ordered via email at: jerry@wildintherockies.com.

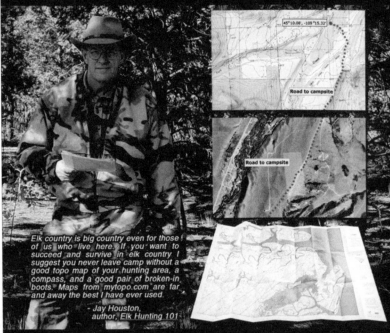

If you have enjoyed reading Elk Hunting 101, or believe that you have gained any measure of value to add to your existing elk hunting skills, I would like to hear from you. My email address is elkmaster@elkcamp.com. I make a personal effort to respond to every email received.

If you are looking for a hunt here in Colorado, whether hunting on your own, or hunting with an Outfitter, I would be glad to help you put this together. Feel free to email me at the email address above.

Our plan for the next book in this series is to have it available sometime in 2005. In Elk Hunting 201 I will be taking a more in depth look at the great adventure of elk hunting. Some of the topics I plan to include are:

- Where to find the big bulls
- Understanding bull to cow ratios and stats
- How to maximize points for the draw
- How to effectively scout public land
- How to find affordable private land hunts
- Mules vs. horses for packing in
- How to successfully hunt the rut
- Elk summer range vs. winter range
- Bowhunting tactics for elk
- An in-depth look at how to get in shape for your elk hunt
- How to set up a first class elk camp
- Elk hunting on a budget
- More stories and tall tales of elk hunting

To reserve your copy of Elk Hunting 201, please email me at the address above and put "Elk Hunting 201 Reservation" in the subject line. Be sure to include your name, mailing address, and the number of books that you would like to reserve. When the book is ready to go to press you will receive an email from us with instruction on placing your order. Thanks.

Elk Hunting 201

Coming in 2005

Reserve Your Copy Today
At
www.elkcamp.com

ElkHuntingMag.com

ElkHuntingmag.com is your online elk hunting magazine, published by elk hunters…for elk hunters. Each quarter we publish a new first-class version of the magazine with new articles, great new photos, new products, and new information. Each quarterly publication will have regularly featured authors and subjects just like print magazines. Also like print magazines, ElkHuntingMag.com will feature products and services from many of the leading names in the hunting industry.

Some of the regular features you can expect to see in upcoming issues include:

- **Bowhunting for Elk**
- **Running' and Gunnin'**
- **Gearing Up For Elk**
- **Outfitter's Camp**
- **Game Preparation and Recipes**
- **Elk Calls and Elk Calling**
- **Land Navigation, Topo Maps, GPS**
- **How and Where to Locate Elk**
- **Elk Hunting Tactics and Strategies**
- **New Product Tests and Evaluations**

Look for us on the web at
www.ElkHuntingMag.com

ELK HUNTING FIELD NOTES

ELK HUNTING FIELD NOTES

ELK HUNTING FIELD NOTES